The Law of Florida Homeowners Associations

Single Family Subdivisions
Townhouse & Cluster Developments
Master Community Associations

6th Edition

by Peter M. Dunbar, Esq.
and Charles F. Dudley, Esq.

Pineapple Press, Inc.
Sarasota, Florida

TILNEY

Inquiries should be addressed to:

Pineapple Press, Inc.
P.O. Box 3889
Sarasota, Florida 34230
www.pineapplepress.com

Library of Congress Cataloging-in-Publication Data

Dunbar, Peter M.
  The law of Florida homeowners associations : single family subdivisions, townhouse & cluster developments, master community associations / Peter M. Dunbar, Charles F. Dudley.—6th ed.
      p. cm.
  Includes bibliographical references and index.
  ISBN 1-56164-325-4 (pbk : alk. paper)
  1. Homeowners' associations—Law and legislation—Florida. I. Dudley, Charles F. II. Title.

  KFF114.C6D865 2004
  346.75904'32—dc22   2004023644

13-digit ISBN 978-1-56164-325-7

Sixth Edition
10 9 8 7 6 5 4 3 2

Printed in the United States of America

About the Authors

Peter M. Dunbar is a partner in the law firm of Pennington, Moore, Wilkinson, Bell & Dunbar, P.A., in Tallahassee, Florida. For a period of almost three years before joining the firm he served in the Office of the Governor of the State of Florida as General Counsel and later as Chief of Staff. Before joining Governor Martinez's staff, he was in private practice and specialized in the areas of real property and community association law. Mr. Dunbar is an Adjunct Professor at Florida State University College of Law and he has taught and lectured on associations and the law governing multi-family living since 1974. He is a member of the Florida Bar and an honors graduate from the College of Law at Florida State University.

Mr. Dunbar served as a member of the Florida House of Representatives for ten years. During his legislative career he served as a member of the House Judiciary Committee and sponsored or co-sponsored every major new law affecting community associations during his decade of service in the Legislature.

Charles F. Dudley is an attorney in private practice in Tallahassee, Florida. In his professional capacity, he is involved on a daily basis with policy makers and administrators in both the legislative and executive branches of Florida's state government. In recent legislative sessions, Mr. Dudley has contributed to the development of the changes in Florida's housing laws for condominiums, cooperatives, mobile homes and homeowners associations. Mr. Dudley also serves as General Counsel to the Florida Cable Telecommunications Association and served as a member of the 1996 Florida Telecommunications Taxation Task Force.

Mr. Dudley is a member of the Florida Bar and an honors graduate from the College of Law at Florida State University. He has been a guest columnist on the law of homeowners associations for *Community Living* and other publications, and he continues to be involved in the pending changes to Florida's housing laws. Mr. Dudley was featured as one of Florida's "Next Wave" of leaders in the December 1993 issue of *Florida Trend* magazine.

Contents

6 RIGHTS AND RESPONSIBILITIES OF THE PARCEL OWNER

7 COVENANTS AND USE OF ASSOCIATION PROPERTY

Introduction

In 1992, special laws governing homeowners associations in Florida were enacted for the first time. In 1995, 1997 and 2004, the special statutory provisions were expanded and refined. Prior to these enactments, the general corporate law of Florida governed the affairs of the corporate associations. In 2000, the special statutory provisions relating to mandatory homeowners associations were assigned to a separate chapter of the Florida Statutes—Chapter 720. Today, the general corporate law and the special homeowners associations provisions harmonize to provide the framework for association operation. This manual is offered as a guide to assist those who are governed by a homeowners association in Florida.

The residents who assume positions of responsibility as officers and directors of homeowners associations will be the key to its success or the catalyst for its failure. The association is created to preserve the concept of planned residential living, and the officers and directors are charged with the responsibility of insuring its success. These responsibilities can be significant and their implementation is governed by formal procedures that may be both new and confusing to community leaders.

Leaders of the homeowners associations are, in almost all cases, volunteers and residents of the community. They are confronted with enforcing the covenants and restrictions among their neighbors and balancing community goals and the rights of individual owners.

The officers and directors carry out their duties within the formal confines of the governing documents, the rules of parliamentary procedure and applicable law. Collectively, these formal standards assure fairness and uniformity for community residents and present a unique challenge to the community leaders. The formalities prescribe notice and require open meetings. They establish eligibility and set standards of conduct for officers and directors, and they provide the methods by which the membership may express its collective will.

Formal policies and procedures do not have to be unnecessarily complicated and they should not frustrate the substantive goals of the homeowners association. This manual is designed as a practical guide to assist community leaders with their duties and responsibilities, and as a reference tool to assure the successful operation of the homeowners association.

This manual provides a step-by-step explanation of the statutory requirements for meetings, membership voting and the parliamentary procedures that govern gatherings of the association and its board of directors. It contains sets of forms and sample documents for use by community leaders, and seeks to provide answers to the basic questions that arise from time to time on the operation of the community.

When officers and directors approach implementation of their duties, the authors hope that this manual will assist them and their advisors with problems of procedure and association organization. It is offered to simplify and clarify the formal and technical elements of association operation. By doing so, the main role of the homeowners association can be successfully carried out and the organization will function correctly for the benefit of its member-residents.

1

The Homeowners Association and the Community Concept

1

1.1 Homeowners Association Concept. Mandatory homeowners associations are the cornerstones for many of Florida's planned residential communities. Properly run, they promote the community concept and protect the community's property values. Under Florida's Land Sales Act, homeowners associations are often assigned significant responsibilities to provide services and to maintain improvements within the community such as roadways and drainage structures.[1] In many cases, homeowners associations make available recreational and other facilities that might not otherwise be affordable or available to homeowners and residents.

Historically, homeowners associations have been organized under the Florida Not For Profit Corporation Act (Chapter 617 of the Florida Statutes) and have operated under the general provisions of corporate law.[2] Although efforts to provide special statutory provisions to govern the operations of mandatory homeowners associations had been attempted for years, it was not until 1992 that these efforts were successful.[3] In 1995, 1997 and 2004, the Legislature expanded the special statutory provisions for the operation of most of Florida's traditional mandatory homeowners associations.[4] In 2000, these special provisions were reassigned to Chapter 720 of the Florida Statutes.[5]

Associations subject to regulation by Chapter 718 (Condominium Act), Chapter 719 (Cooperative Act), Chapter 721 (Florida Vacation Plan and Time-Sharing Act), and Chapter 723 (Florida Mobile Home Act) are not governed by the special homeowners association provisions in Chapter 720 of the

---

[1] Chapter 498, F.S.

[2] §617.002, F.S.

[3] The Residential Planned Development Study Commission, "Report to the Florida Legislature," at 1 (Jan. 24, 1985) (on file at the Florida Legislative Library).

[4] Chapter 2004-345, *Laws of Florida.*

[5] Chapter 2000-258, *Laws of Florida.* The sections are subject to renumbering by Statutory Revision in 2004.

Florida Statutes. Associations governing communities that are comprised of property primarily intended for commercial, industrial or other non-residential use are also exempt from the special provisions in the law governing mandatory homeowners associations.[6]

For all other homeowners associations responsible for the operation of a community where membership is a mandatory condition for the owners of property upon which assessments are required and may become a lien on the parcel, the homeowners association provisions of Chapter 720 of the Florida Statutes apply.[7] The statutory scheme of Chapter 720 is comprehensive and a county or city may not enact an ordinance imposing additional or more stringent requirements for homeowners associations.[8]

1.2 Applicable Law and Legislative Intent. While other parts of the corporate law found in Chapter 617 of the Florida Statutes affect mandatory homeowners associations in Florida, Chapter 720 of the Florida Statutes gives special recognition to those corporations that operate residential communities in the state. These designated sections of Chapter 720 set out specific operational procedures for homeowners associations while providing for the protection of individual rights of association members.[9]

In its enactment of these special sections of the law in 1995, the Legislature also made a series of basic findings concerning the law of Florida homeowners associations. First, the law is intended to protect the rights of property owners and association members without unduly impairing the association's ability to perform its functions. Next, the contract rights creat-

---

6 §720.302 (3), F.S.
7 §720.301 (8) and (11), F.S.
8 Advisory Opinion of the Florida Attorney General, AGO 2001-01.
9 §720.302 (1), F.S.

ed for the benefit of the association and its members in the declaration of covenants governing the community are not to be impaired by the law. And finally, the Legislature determined that it was not in the best interests of either the homeowners association or its members to create an agency of government to regulate association affairs.[10]

1.3 The Community. The "community" under Chapter 720 of the Florida Statutes includes all of the real property that is, or will be, subject to the declaration of covenants governing the property. Included in the statutory definition of "community" are not only the common areas owned or leased by the association but also those lands and leaseholds that are subject to the jurisdiction of the homeowners association including the lots, parcels or tracts of individual owners.[11]

A "parcel," lot or tract is the real property within the community that is subject to separate conveyance and exclusive ownership. The parcel may be either platted or unplatted and its owner, or an association in which the owner is a member, must be required to pay homeowners association assessments that, if not paid, may result in a lien against the parcel.[12]

Common areas and recreational facilities serving a homeowners association and its members are also included within the definition of the community. The common areas may be owned or leased by the association, or they may be dedicated to the association or its members by recorded plat.[13] The common areas serving the community must be made available to parcel owners and their invited guests to use as the property was intended.[14]

---

[10] §720.302 (1) and (2), F.S.

[11] §720.301 (3), F.S.

[12] §720.301 (11), F.S.

[13] §720.301 (2), F.S.; *see also* §177.081, F.S.

[14] *Blue Reef Holding Corp., Inc. v. Coyne*, 545 So.2d 1053 (Fla. 4th DCA 1994); *Lewis v. S & T Anchorage, Inc.*, 616 So.2d 478 (Fla. 3d DCA 1993).

A parcel owner's right to assemble in the common areas or in the facilities cannot be unreasonably restricted, and an owner may enforce his or her right to use the common area through mediation and in court.[15] (See 6.2.) The association also has a responsibility to protect those who use and occupy the common areas of the community from foreseeable hazards.[16]

1.4 The Homeowners Association. The corporate entity responsible for the operation of the community created by the declaration of covenants is known as the "homeowners association," or simply as the "association."[17] In Florida, it is permissible, and not uncommon, to find that the homeowners association operates more than one community.[18] The association must be a Florida corporation, and its voting membership must be made up of the parcel owners in the community or their designated agents.[19] It is permissible for the homeowners association to have more than one class of members.[20]

Membership in the association is a mandatory condition of parcel ownership in the community, and the association is authorized to impose assessments against its members that, if unpaid, may become a lien against the parcel owned by the member.[21] Each homeowners association is authorized by

---

[15] §720.304 (1), F.S.

[16] *Barrwood Homeowners Ass'n, Inc. v. Maser,* 675 So.2d 983 (Fla. 4th DCA 1996); *Sanzare v. Varesi,* 681 So.2d 785 (Fla. 4th DCA 1996).

[17] §720.301 (7), F.S. The term "homeowners association" does not include a community development district or other special taxing district created pursuant to statute. Homeowners association members may, however, be subject to a special taxing district. *See Chambless v. The Officers and Directors of Snapper Creek,* 743 So.2d 129 (Fla. 3d DCA 1999).

[18] §720.302 (1), F.S.

[19] §720.301 (8), F.S.

[20] §720.303 (1), F.S.

[21] §720.301 (1) and (8), F.S.

statute to enforce the covenants and restrictions contained in the governing documents of the community. If the governing documents permit, the association may also suspend the rights of a parcel owner to use the common areas of the community for a violation of the restrictions in the governing documents.[22] (See 7.5.)

1.5 Assessments. To fund the operations, amenities and special needs of a homeowners association, each parcel owner is required to contribute a proportionate share of the costs and expenses.[23] Each owner's proportionate share of the annual budget and the general operations and obligations of the association is referred to in statute as an "assessment" or an "amenity fee." The assessments or amenity fees may be payable to the association, to the developer or to another owner of property serving the community. Under the statutes and the documents governing the community, any fees or assessments remaining unpaid by a parcel owner may become a lien on the parcel until the assessment is paid.[24] (See 5.9.)

The purposes for which a homeowners association may levy a charge or an assessment against a parcel must be identified in the articles of incorporation, bylaws or other documents governing the community.[25] The homeowners association is required to maintain a current account and a periodic statement of the account for each member of the association. The account must designate the member's name, the due date and amount of

---

[22] §720.305 (1) and (2), F.S.

[23] §720.308, F.S.; *see also Wood v. McElvey*, 296 So.2d 102 (Fla. 2d DCA 1974).

[24] §720.301 (1), F.S.; *see also Bennett v. Behring Corp.*, 466 F. Supp. 689 (S.D. Fla. 1979) holding that the constitutional protection of homestead does not necessarily invalidate a debt or lien but may under certain circumstances take priority.

[25] *Wenger v. Breakwater Homeowners' Ass'n*, 423 So.2d 619, 621 (Fla. 4th DCA 1982), *citing Orlando Orange Grove Co. v. Hale*, 107 Fla. 304, 311, 144 So. 674, 676 (1932) holding a corporation may only exercise those powers conferred by the articles of incorporation or those powers necessary to carry out authorized functions.

each assessment, the amount paid upon the account and the balance due.[26]

1.6 Declaration of Covenants. A covenant is a commitment, agreement or contract which grants a right or imposes a liability.[27] The recorded documents in each community include many such rights, liabilities and commitments governing the use and occupancy of the property governed by the homeowners association. The documents containing these rights, liabilities and commitments, i.e., the restrictive covenants or deed restrictions, are defined in Chapter 720 of the Florida Statutes as the "declaration of covenants" or "declaration" for the community.[28]

The recorded declaration of covenants for the community "runs with the land" as a set of permanent restrictions governing its use. The restrictions are equitable rights arising out of the contractual relationship between and among the parcel owners in the community.[29] The restrictions and covenants subject the community to the jurisdiction and control of the homeowners association, and they remain effective until the covenants and restrictions are terminated or until they are found to be no longer necessary.[30] While the declaration of covenants is in

---

26 §720.303 (4) (j) 2., F.S.

27 *Black's Law Dictionary*, 5th Ed. Rev.; *see generally Venetian Isles Homeowners Assoc., Inc. v. Albrecht*, 823 So.2d 813 (Fla. 2d DCA 2002); *Regency Highland Associates v. Sherwood*, 388 So.2d 271 (Fla. 4th DCA 1980), *rev. den.*, 397 So.2d 778 and *Balzer v. Indian Lake Maintenance, Inc.*, 346 So.2d 146 (Fla. 2d DCA 1977).

28 §720.301 (4), F.S.; *see also Voight v. Harbour Heights Improvement Ass'n*, 218 So.2d 803, 806 (Fla. 4th DCA 1969).

29 *Cudjoe Gardens Property Owners Assoc., Inc. v. Payne*, 779 So.2d 598 (Fla. 3d DCA 2001).

30 §720.301 (4), F.S.; *see also Crissman v. Dedakis*, 330 So.2d 103 (Fla. 1st DCA 1976); *Bartow v. Moline Properties*, 121 Fla. 683, 164 So.551 (Fla. 1935) holding that when covenants lack an expressed expiration, a reasonable time limitation is implied.

effect, the provisions are enforceable by and against each parcel owner.[31] (See 7.4 and 7.5.)

When covenants run with the land, a person who assumes ownership of a parcel of the land also assumes ownership with the presumed knowledge of the covenants.[32] In other words, each new parcel owner is presumed to know and understand the content of the documents governing the homeowners association and the community. It is the responsibility of the original developer to supply copies of the governing documents to initial purchasers, and it is the seller's responsibility to do so if the sale is by an owner who is not the developer. These disclosures must be made prior to the execution of a contract for sale.[33] (See 6.8.)

The recorded declaration of covenants for the community may include the articles of incorporation and bylaws for the homeowners association, or they may incorporate them by reference. The declaration of covenants together with all duly adopted and recorded amendments and exhibits as well as the articles of incorporation and the bylaws for the association are known as the "governing documents" for the community.[34] Together, the governing documents combine to set out both the powers and the limitations on the powers of the homeowners association.[35]

In communities created after October 1, 1998, the law prohibits the inclusion of certain provisions in the governing

---

[31] §720.305 (1), F.S.; *see also Loch Haven Homeowners' Ass'n v. Nelle*, 389 So.2d 697 (Fla. 2d DCA 1980), *affirmed*, 413 So.2d 28 (1982).

[32] *Hagan v. Sabal Palms, Inc.*, 186 So.2d 302, 312-13 (Fla. 2d DCA 1966).

[33] §21, Chapter 2004-345, *Laws of Florida.*

[34] §720.301 (6), F.S. *See Highland Lakes Prop. Owners v. Schlack*, 724 So.2d 621 (Fla. 5th DCA 1998).

[35] *See S & T Anchorage, Inc. v. Lewis*, 575 So.2d 696 (Fla. 3d DCA 1991), reminding us that an association, like any other corporation, is prohibited from performing *ultra vires* acts.

document for the community. In the event such provisions do appear in the covenants, the statute declares them to be unenforceable. Among the provisions that are not permitted are (1) the unilateral right of the developer to make changes to the community's documents after transition; (2) limitations or restrictions on the right of the homeowners association to sue the developer; and (3) provisions purporting to give weighted voting rights to the developer after transitions.[36] Each of these provisions, as well as variations of each, is declared to be null and void as a matter of public policy.[37]

1.7 Articles of Incorporation. The articles of incorporation, or corporate charter, is the document which establishes the homeowners association.[38] The term "articles of incorporation" includes the original document creating the association and all amendments to it and any other documents which define the existing form, membership and responsibility of the homeowners association. For example, the definition also includes articles of consolidation or articles of merger if several homeowners associations have been combined into a single organization.[39] The articles of incorporation enumerate the powers with which the homeowners association is vested, and its powers are limited to those specifically expressed, and those implied powers necessary to perform the authorized functions of the association.[40]

The articles of incorporation may establish a corporation for profit or a corporation not-for-profit to be the homeowners association. Under most circumstances the articles of incorpo-

---

[36] §720.3075 (1), F.S.

[37] §720.3075 (2), F.S.

[38] §617.0202, F.S.

[39] §617.01401 (1), F.S.

[40] *S & T Anchorage, Inc. v. Lewis, supra* note 32; *Wenger v. Breakwater Homeowners' Ass'n*, 423 So.2d 619 (Fla. 4th DCA 1982).

ration establish a "corporation not-for-profit" under Chapter 617 of the Florida Statutes. A corporation not-for-profit is not tax exempt, but it is a corporation where no part of the income may be distributed to the members, directors or officers of the association.[41] Every corporation not-for-profit has all of the powers granted by the Florida Not For Profit Corporation Act (Chapter 617 of the Florida Statutes) except as otherwise limited by the articles of incorporation themselves.[42] The articles of incorporation become effective and the homeowners association may begin to operate when the articles are filed with the Division of Corporations.[43]

1.8 Bylaws. The articles of incorporation of the homeowners association define the association's basic structure and its areas of responsibility. The bylaws establish the procedures for carrying out these responsibilities. They define the powers and the manner for exercising those powers by the board of directors and by each of the homeowners association's officers. Stated differently, the operation of the association is governed by the bylaws of the association.[44]

When creating the bylaws, there is a substantial amount of discretion available to establish the specific procedures which the homeowners association will follow. There are some provisions in the law, however, that mandate specific operational procedures for the association, and the bylaws must be consistent with these statutory requirements. Among these requirements are restrictions on the use of proxies, financial reporting obligations by the association, the requirement that all

---

[41] §617.01401 (5), F.S.

[42] §617.0302, F.S.; *Orlando Orange Grove Co. v. Hale, supra* note 23.

[43] §617.0203 (1), F.S. For associations created after October 1, 1995, the governing documents must be recorded in the official records of the county in which the community is located. §720.303 (1), F.S.

[44] §617.01401 (3) and §617.0206, F.S.

board meetings be open to the members of the association and the requirement that notice be posted for all board meetings. The law also requires that certain records of the association be open to parcel owners.[45] Because a portion of these mandatory requirements may not physically be within the bylaws, the board of directors and the association officers must be aware that portions of the operational requirements may be found in the statute and not as a part of the bylaws actually attached to the homeowners association documents.

1.9   Rules and Regulations. The supplemental restrictions authorized by the association bylaws and statute are traditionally referred to as the "rules and regulations." They are common in other forms of planned residential communities such as condominiums, cooperatives and mobile home parks, and their role in homeowners associations is recognized by the statute.[46] The bylaws of the association may provide for the authority to adopt the rules and regulations and may set out the procedures to follow when adopting them.[47] The law governing homeowners associations specifically authorizes the adoption of rules governing the access to the official records of the association,[48] the taping and videotaping of meetings of the membership and the board of directors,[49] and the right of members to speak at meetings of the board of directors.[50]

The rules and regulations of the homeowners association are similar to the recorded declaration of covenants, but they are not clothed with the strong presumption of validity and enforce-

---

[45]   §720.303, F.S.

[46]   *See* §720.303 (4) (e) and §720.304 (1), F.S.

[47]   §617.01401 (3) and §617.0206, F.S.

[48]   §720.303 (5) (c), F.S.

[49]   §720.306 (10), F.S.

[50]   §720.303 (2)(b), F.S.

ability that accompany recorded restrictions.[51] The rules of the homeowners association are considered a part of its official records,[52] and the law requires a standard of reasonableness to ensure their enforceability.[53]

1.10 Priority and Consistency of the Documents. Each of the documents which make up the governing documents of the community and support the operation of the homeowners association are designed to interrelate and compliment each other for the benefit of association members and parcel owners. Each of these documents should be consistent with the others and should be interpreted to carry out the common scheme of the community.[54] When an apparent inconsistency is identified within a single document or between two of the governing documents, the inconsistent provisions should be interpreted in such a way as to leave both provisions in effect and consistent with one another.[55]

When it is not possible to resolve an inconsistency between two different documents governing the community,

---

[51] *See Eastpointe Property Owners' Ass'n v. Cohen*, 505 So.2d 518, 520 (Fla. 4th DCA 1987) where actions by the board of directors were deemed valid provided they were not prohibited by the articles of incorporation or bylaws and were deemed reasonable actions designed to further the community concept. *See also Bay Island Towers, Inc. v. Bay Island-Siesta Ass'n*, 316 So.2d 574 (Fla. 2d DCA 1975).

[52] §720.303 (4) (e), F.S.

[53] §720.304 (1), F.S.; *see also Eastpointe Property Owners' Ass'n v. Cohen, supra* note 45.

[54] *Holiday Pines Prop. Owners v. Wetherington*, 596 So.2d 84, 87 (Fla. 4th DCA 1992).

[55] "A restrictive covenant must be read in the context of the entire document in which it is contained." *Franklin v. White Egret Condominium, Inc.*, 358 So.2d 1084, 1087 (Fla. 4th DCA 1977). *See also Flamingo Ranch Estates, Inc. v. Sunshine Ranches Homeowners, Inc.*, 303 So.2d 665 (Fla. 4th DCA 1974).

then the provision in the highest priority document will prevail.[56] The document with the highest priority is the declaration of covenants, and its provisions will prevail over inconsistent provisions in other documents.[57] In descending order, the articles of incorporation for the homeowners association have the next highest priority after the declaration. They are followed in descending order by the bylaws of the association and the duly adopted rules and regulations.[58] When a provision in any of the documents is inconsistent with state, federal or local laws, the inconsistency in the community documents is invalidated in favor of the law.

1.11 Minutes and Records. A record of all meetings of the membership and the board of directors must be made in a businesslike manner and in written form or in a form that is capable of being converted to a written format within a reasonable period of time.[59] The board of directors is the custodian of all the official records of the homeowners association including all meeting minutes.

The official records consist of all of the documents creating and governing the homeowners association. These include copies of plans, permits, warranties and other items provided by the developer. They include the articles of incorporation, bylaws, deed restrictions and the current rules and regulations governing the community. The official records include the accounting and financial records of the association and all con-

---

[56] *Koplowitz v. Imperial Towers Condominium, Inc.*, 478 So.2d 504 (Fla. 4th DCA 1985); *San Souci v. Division of Fla. Land Sales and Condominiums*, 421 So.2d 623 (Fla. 1st DCA 1982).

[57] *S & T Anchorage, Inc. v. Lewis, supra* note 32.

[58] *Beachwood Villas Condominium v. Poor*, 448 So.2d 1143 (Fla. 4th DCA 1984); *Hidden Harbour Estates, Inc. v. Basso*, 393 So.2d 637 (Fla. 4th DCA 1981).

[59] §720.303 (3), F.S.; *see also Fletcher's Cyclopedia on Corporations*, Corporate Meetings and Elections, §2012.

tracts, management agreements and leases to which the association is a party or under which it is obligated. The records also include the association insurance policies and a current roster of parcel owners.[60]

The board of directors must ensure that the minutes and other records of the homeowners association are properly maintained and available for inspection by the members and their authorized representatives. (See 6.6.) The minutes of the membership meetings, meetings of the board of directors and most other records of the association must be maintained for a minimum period of seven (7) years.[61]

1.12 Community Association Management. The managers of homeowners associations having fifty (50) or more parcels or having an annual budget of $100,000.00 or more are required to be licensed by the Department of Business and Professional Regulation.[62] To be certified as a community association manager, an individual must demonstrate good moral character and pass an examination administered by the Department prior to obtaining a license. The Department sets the standards for the application, examination and revocation of the licenses for those who wish to serve as managers of residential communities in Florida. A licensed residential community manager is required to participate in the continuing education prescribed by the Department in order to be eligible for renewal of the license.[63]

"Community association management" includes activities for remuneration involving the control and disbursement of funds, the preparation of budgets or other financial documents,

---

[60] §720.303 (3), F.S.
[61] *Id.*[62]§468.431 (2), F.S.
[62] §468.431
[63] *See generally,* §468.433, F.S. and §61B-55.006, F.A.C.

assistance with the notice and conduct of association meetings, coordination of maintenance for the residential development and other day-to-day services. A person who performs clerical or ministerial functions under the direct supervision and control of a licensed manager does not need to be licensed. A person charged only with performing the maintenance of a homeowners association who does not assist in any management activities also does not need to be licensed by the Department.[64]

1.13 Automated External Defibrillator. A homeowners association is permitted to maintain an automated external defibrillator device in the community for use in medical emergencies, and the association is immune from liability when the device is used as long as it is properly maintained, appropriate training has been provided to association employees, and the local emergency medical services director has been notified of the placement of the device in the community.[65] If the defibrillator device is placed in the community, the association's insurer may not require the association to purchase medical malpractice insurance and cannot exclude the use of the device from coverage under the association's general liability insurance coverage.[66]

1.14 Construction Defects—Presuit Procedures. Construction defect claims against a developer, contractor, or design professional for damages to a single-family home, a multifamily residential building, or the common areas and improvements serving the community must be submitted to presuit procedures before a claim can be filed in court. The procedures provide the opportunity to resolve the dispute to the satis-

---

[64] §468.431 (2), F.S.
[65] §768.1325 (3), F.S.
[66] §768.1325 (6), F.S.

faction of the affected owners or the association by correcting the defects or by the payment of a cash settlement.

Notice of a defect claim must be served on the developer, contractor, or design professional at least 60 days before a court action is filed. The notice must describe the claim in detail, and the contractor of design professional must be given an opportunity to inspect the defect and has 30 days to provide a written response to the claim. The response must be in writing, and it may (1) offer to fix the defect at no cost to the homeowners; (2) offer to settle the claim by a monetary payment together with a timetable for making the payment; or (3) dispute the claim and refuse to correct the alleged defect.[67]

If the developer, contractor, or design professional does not respond on time or settle claim, the homeowner or the association making the claim may proceed with a court action. The homeowner or the association making the claim may also reject the settlement offer in writing and proceed in court without further notice.[68]

Before commencing any court action against any party in the name of the homeowners association, including an action based upon construction defects, involving amounts in controversy in excess of $100,000, the association must obtain the affirmative approval of a majority of the homeowners at a meeting of the membership at which a quorum is present.[69]

---

[67] The time periods for claims in multifamily structures containing more than 20 dwelling units are longer.

[68] §§558.01 through 558.005, F.S.

[69] §720.303(1), F.S.

2

Meetings of the Membership

2.1   General. Membership meetings are an essential part of a successfully operating homeowners association. The membership meetings provide association members the opportunity to select community leaders and a forum to adopt and approve association financial policies, make changes in the governing documents, handle items of special business involving the membership and address other matters for the general welfare of the community.

If proper procedures are implemented and followed, membership meetings can deal with the most controversial subjects and still end with productive results. Unless the association bylaws provide a lower number, thirty (30) percent of the voting interests in the homeowners association must be present at a meeting to constitute a quorum.[1] For purposes of establishing a quorum, parcel owners attending in person and by general and limited proxy may be counted,[2] although the participation of those represented by proxy is restricted. (See 2.5.)

In some circumstances, owners may take action by written agreement, without a meeting, when it is expressly permitted by the articles of incorporation, the bylaws or the law requiring the action. In all other cases, actions requiring parcel owner approval must take place at meetings of the association membership that are properly called and conducted.[3]

2.2   Annual and Regular Meetings. All homeowners associations are required to hold at least one regular membership meeting each year. This meeting is referred to as the "annual meeting," and the date, time and place for it will likely be set forth in the bylaws of the association, or it will be set by the

---

[1]   §720.306 (1), F.S.
[2]   §720.306 (1) and (8), F.S.
[3]   §617.0701 (4), F.S.

board of directors in the manner required in the bylaws and consistent with the requirements of Chapter 720 of the Florida Statutes.[4] (See 2.4.)

A well-planned annual meeting will maximize the opportunities to provide information to members of the association and to receive their input, suggestions and complaints. The annual meeting of members often presents the only periodic opportunity that individual owners have to review the affairs of their homeowners association, and any and all proper business of the association can be transacted at the annual meeting. Unless otherwise provided in the governing documents of the association, the election of directors must be held at, or in conjunction with, the annual meeting of the membership.[5] (See 2.10.)

2.3 Special Meetings. From time to time, members of the homeowners association or the board of directors may find it necessary to hold special members meetings. Special meetings are limited in their scope and purpose, and the notice to the members for a special meeting must include a description of the purpose for which the meeting is called.[6]

A special meeting of the association membership must be held when called by the board of directors or when at least ten (10) percent of the total voting interests of the association request a special meeting unless a different percentage of the membership is stated in the governing documents. The business conducted at a special meeting of the members is limited to the purpose or purposes described in the notice for the meeting.[7]

---

[4]   §720.306 (2), F.S.
[5]   §720.306 (2) and (9), F.S.
[6]   §720.306 (4), F.S.
[7]   §720.306 (2), F.S.

2.4   Content of Meeting Notice. Notice of all membership meetings of the homeowners association must be mailed, delivered or electronically transmitted to the members not less than fourteen (14) days prior to the meeting, and an affidavit executed by the person providing the notice must be filed with the records of the association as evidence that the notice was given as required.[8] (See Form 8.11.) The notice for a membership meeting, whether annual or special, must contain the date, time and place at which the meeting will be held.[9] If the meeting is a special meeting, the notice must include a description of the purpose or purposes for which the meeting has been called.[10] The notice of meeting must be electronically transmitted or mailed with postage paid to the address of each member shown in the association's records,[11] and the notice is effective when mailed.[12]

In a well-run community, the giving of notice will include, at minimum, the notice, an agenda of the business to be covered and a proxy form for the convenience of members who cannot attend in person. As a final option, the notice can be accompanied by reports of committees, reports by the association's president or reports by the management company. If amendments to the governing documents are to be considered at the meeting, then copies of the amendments should be included with the notice. Finally, it may be helpful to include a general letter of explanation about the business to be discussed at the membership meeting and procedures to be followed during the course of the meeting.

The notice of each meeting is given by or at the direction of the president, secretary or other officer or person assigned

---

8   §720.306 (5), F.S.
9   §720.306 (2) and (4), F.S.
10   §720.306 (4), F.S.
11   §617.0141 (1), F.S.
12   §617.0141 (3), F.S.

the responsibility of providing notice.[13] Notice of a meeting can be waived by a written waiver of notice either before or after a meeting. Attendance of a member at a meeting, either in person or by proxy, constitutes a waiver of notice unless the member attends solely for purpose of objecting, at the beginning of the meeting, to the lack of notice or the transaction of business at the meeting.[14]

2.5 Proxies. The bylaws for most homeowners associations permit absent parcel owners to participate and vote in membership meetings by proxy. Florida law also authorizes the use of proxies by a parcel owner but places certain restrictions on their use. No proxy is valid for more than ninety (90) days, and a proxy may be used only at the meeting for which it was given and any lawfully adjourned meetings thereof.[15] (See 2.14.) The proxy may be general in nature or very limited, restricting the person designated to vote it and allowing little discretion when representing the absent member. Proxies are authorized for purposes of determining the presence of a quorum at all meetings of the membership,[16] and, unless otherwise restricted by the association bylaws, the use of proxies is permitted in the election of directors.[17] (See 2.10.)

To be valid, the proxy must identify the person who will vote the proxy at the meeting. The identification may be made by name or by designating a specific officer of the association, such as the president or secretary. The proxy must (1) be dated, (2) state the date, time and place of the meeting for which the proxy is given, and (3) be signed by the person who is authorized to grant the proxy.[18] A proxy is revocable at any time at the pleasure of the person who executes it, and if the proxy form

---

[13] §720.303 (1) and §720.306 (2) and (3), F.S.
[14] §617.0701 (5) (a) and (b), F.S.
[15] §720.306 (7) and (8), F.S.
[16] §720.306 (1), F.S.
[17] §720.306 (9), F.S.
[18] §720.306 (8), F.S.

expressly permits, any proxy holder may appoint, in writing, a substitute to act in place of the proxy holder.[19]

The bylaws of most homeowners associations require that the proxies be returned to the secretary or other officer of the association prior to the meeting. The appointment of a proxy is effective when received by the secretary or other officer authorized to tabulate votes. An executed telegram or cablegram transmitted by a voting member of the association or a photographic, photostatic, facsimile, or equivalent reproduction of a proxy form is a sufficient proxy.[20]

2.6 Conducting the Meeting. Conducting a fair and successful membership meeting is the responsibility of the presiding officer or chairman. The chairman must set and maintain the proper tenor for the meeting and, as chairman, must at all times be fair, impartial and neutral on each issue that comes before the meeting. The goal of the chairman should be to conduct an open and impartial membership meeting without regard to the outcome on specific votes or motions.[21]

In addition to setting an example of basic courtesy and fairness, the chairman must also be familiar with proper parliamentary procedures used for conducting the membership meeting. By following proper procedures, the chairman can allow the meeting to proceed with full participation of all members but without argument or disruption.[22] Conducting a successful

---

19 *Id.* [20] §607.0722 (2), F.S.

21 "Aside from express regulations, all that is necessary is that the meeting be conducted by the proper persons, with fairness and good faith towards all who are entitled to take part, and in such a way as to enable them to express their vote upon questions coming before the meeting." *Fletcher's Cyclopedia on Corporations*, Corporate Meetings and Elections, §2012.

22 *Abbey Properties Co., Inc. v. Presidential Insurance Co.*, 119 So.2d 74, 77 (Fla. 2d DCA 1960); 18A *Am. Jur.* 2d, Corporations, §986.

meeting requires the assurance that all members wishing to participate can do so and that members wishing to make motions or debate an issue will have the appropriate opportunity.

Debate or remarks by individual members is protected by law[23] and should be limited or cut off only in extreme circumstances or when the remarks are being made at an improper point on the agenda. It is not unusual to find one or more individual members who will attempt to be disruptive, either intentionally or because they feel strongly on a particular issue. In such circumstances, the chairman must remain courteous, patient and composed. The disruptive member desiring to be heard should be guided to the correct part of the agenda for his or her remarks and advised how to make them in an appropriate and dignified fashion.[24] (See 2.11 and 2.12.)

2.7   Debate. Debate begins after a motion has been made, seconded and stated by the presiding officer to the membership meeting. Each individual desiring to debate a motion must first be recognized by the chairman of the meeting.[25] If *Robert's Rules of Order Newly Revised* is being used, no member may speak more than a total of ten minutes on any single issue. A member is not permitted to speak a second time on the issue until all persons desiring to be heard the first time have had an opportunity to speak. The meeting chairman may bring debate to a close after the matter under consideration has been reasonably discussed if the strict rules of parliamentary procedure are not being followed.[26]

---

[23] §720.306 (6), F.S.

[24] To be valid, procedures must be reasonable and not arbitrary, and they must not be unreasonable in their practical application. *See Conlee Construction Co. v. Cay Construction Co.*, 221 So.2d 792, 796-797 (Fla. 4th DCA 1969).

[25] *Robert's Rules of Order Newly Revised* (1990), §42.

[26] Fletcher's Cyclopedia on Corporations, Corporate Meetings and Elections, §2012.

Members' debate must be confined to the specific issue before the meeting. Debate must be presented in a respectful manner so as to avoid issues of personalities and personal attacks. The maker of the motion, or the person presenting the subject, is the member allowed to speak last, but each member who has followed the proper procedures has the right to speak for at least three (3) minutes on any item.[27] No debate on a motion is in order after the vote has been taken and announced by the presiding officer and the item is no longer under consideration. During debate, it is permissible for a member to ask questions when another person is debating the issue, but all questions must be asked through the chairman. If the speaker is willing to yield to the question, then the member desiring to ask the question may do so.[28]

All main motions properly seconded are debatable as are motions to postpone a matter indefinitely and motions to rescind an action or to ratify an action. A motion to reconsider is debatable if the motion which is being reconsidered was debatable at the time it was made. Motions and matters of privilege, motions to waive the rules, motions to adjourn and to recess and certain other incidental and subsidiary motions are not debatable.[29]

2.8   Matters Out of Order. The bylaws for many homeowners associations specifically adopt *Robert's Rules of Order* for use at association meetings. If the bylaws do not do so, the board of directors or membership may specify the rules of procedure to be followed. The rules of parliamentary procedure establish an order for business of the meeting and the manner in which business is presented and disposed of by those in atten-

---

[27] §720.306 (6), F.S.

[28] *Robert's Rules of Order Newly Revised* (1990), §3.

[29] *Robert's Rules of Order Newly Revised* (1990), Charts, Tables and Lists, §II.

dance at the meeting. The rules of parliamentary procedure also establish an order of priority for motions that may be made by a participant at a meeting. A matter can be out of order when it is presented at the wrong time[30] or when it is presented in the wrong way.[31] Under either of these circumstances, it is the prerogative and the duty of the presiding officer to rule the matter out of order.

A main motion is out of order when another main motion is already pending or when the main motion is on a subject which should arise under a different order of business on the agenda. A motion will also be out of order when a motion of higher priority or of "higher dignity" is already being considered by the meeting. A member may be out of order if the member is either not properly recognized by the chairman or if the member seeks to make a dilatory or frivolous motion.

To call a point of order to demand that the proper order of business be followed is a privileged matter or motion for any member. When claiming a point of order, it is proper for the member to rise and state the point. It does not require a second to be considered by the chairman. A question or point of order cannot be amended by another member and must be decided by the presiding officer without debate.[32]

The presiding officer may seek consultation with the meeting's legal advisor or parliamentarian before ruling on the point of order, but it is the presiding officer's duty to enforce the rules and the order of business of the meeting without debate or unnecessary delay.[33] It is the right of every member who notices

---

[30] *Robert's Rules of Order Newly Revised* (1990), §40.

[31] *Robert's Rules of Order Newly Revised* (1990), §5.

[32] *Robert's Rules of Order Newly Revised* (1990), §23.

[33] *Id.*

a departure from the rules or from the order of business to insist upon proper enforcement.[34]

2.9 Voting and Vote Tabulations. Each member of the homeowners association is assigned a "voting interest" in the association pursuant to the governing documents of the association.[35] The process of voting is the method of expressing the collective will of these membership interests in the affairs of the homeowners association.[36] There are five basic ways for that voting process to take place; (1) by "general consent," (2) by "voice vote," (3) by "show of hands," (4) by "roll call," and (5) by "ballot."[37] Each type of voting has its appropriate place at a membership meeting, and each type can be used effectively at a well run meeting of the members.[38] Use of an inappropriate voting method, on the other hand, can result in disruption or in an actual breakdown of the meeting.

Voting by "general consent" is most often used when there is no objection to an issue before the membership. The chairman of the meeting will simply ask if there is any objection to the motion on the floor, and, if there is none, the chairman will declare that the motion is approved. "Voice voting" is used when an issue before the meeting is relatively non-contro-

---

34 *Id.*; *See also Hagan v. Sabal Palms, Inc.*, 186 So.2d 302 (Fla. 2d DCA 1966) and *Loch Haven Homeowners' Ass'n v. Nelle*, 389 So.2d 697 (Fla. 2d DCA 1980) recognizing an individual homeowner's standing to challenge board action or to enforce covenants.

35 §720.301 (13), F.S.

36 18A *Am. Jur.* 2d, Corporations, §999; "Corporations must be allowed to function under majority control, so long as the majority does no actual wrong to the minority or to others." *Coleman v. Plantation Golf Club, Inc.*, 212 So.2d 806, 808 (Fla. 4th DCA 1968).

37 *Robert's Rules of Order Newly Revised* (1990), §44.

38 The procedural requirements governing the association's role on behalf of its members are appropriately political matters to be addressed within the organization and political framework of the association. *See Eberwein v. Coral Pine Condominium One*, 431 So.2d 616, 618 (Fla. 4th DCA 1983).

versial. The chairman of the meeting will ask for those in favor of the issue to say "aye" and for those who are opposed to the motion to say "no." The chairman will then rule on which group carried the motion. A voice vote should be taken only when the motion requires a majority vote, and, if a member disagrees with the ruling of the chairman on the voice vote, the member may request a count by one of the other voting methods.[39]

Voting by "show of hands" is often a simple sight verification of a voice vote and does not necessarily require that an actual count of hands be made. An exact count of the hands can be made, but an exact count by either roll call or by ballot is more correct. A "roll call" vote requires that the name of each member present be called, allowing for a response of "yes" or "no" to be made on the issue. Because a roll call vote is both time consuming and tedious, it is rarely used at association meetings. Voting by "ballot" is the preferred alternative when an exact vote tabulation is desired.[40]

The final results when voting by general consent, by voice vote or by a show of hands is determined by the chairman of the meeting.[41] Tabulation of a roll call is a simple summation of the individual responses of members, while determining the results from a vote by ballot is by a separate, organized counting procedure which can be simplified significantly if the board has properly organized for the count. When counting, a ballot containing votes for too many board members must be disal-

---

[39] 18A *Am. Jur.* 2d, Corporations, §991.

[40] 18A *Am. Jur.* 2d, Corporations, §1000.

[41] "[A] presiding officer cannot wrongfully declare the result of a vote or arbitrarily refuse to entertain or put motions. Moreover, a chairman's announcement of the results of an election contrary to the vote actually cast has no legal effect on the result." 18A *Am. Jur.* 2d, Corporations, §991.

lowed, while a ballot that does not vote for all available choices is counted for the choices actually made.[42]

When deciding who will actually tabulate the ballots at a membership meeting, the board should keep in mind two basic considerations. The first consideration is the number of votes to be cast and the number of individuals that will be needed to ensure a prompt and accurate tabulation of the votes. The second consideration is the nature of the election and the issues involved. It is helpful to have representatives of both sides of controversial issues involved in the count to remove any doubt on the validity of the results. On some occasions, inspectors of election are actually elected by the membership, but, in most circumstances, the inspectors may simply be appointed by the chairman of the meeting.[43]

Generally, voting and voting rights are covered by the association's bylaws; however, bylaw provisions that conflict with provisions of Florida law are invalid.[44]

2.10 Election of the Board of Directors. The election of the board of directors of the homeowners association is required to be held at, or in conjunction with, the annual meeting of members.[45] All members of the association are eligible to serve on the board of directors, and any member may nominate himself or herself as a candidate for the board of directors at the meeting where the election is to be held.[46]

---

[42] *Fletcher's Cyclopedia on Corporations*, Corporate Meetings and Elections, §2017.

[43] *Fletcher's Cyclopedia on Corporations*, Corporate Meetings and Elections, §2018; 18A *Am. Jur.* 2d, Corporations, §1008 and §1009.

[44] *C.A. Cavendes, Sociedad Financiera v. Florida National Banks*, 566 F. Suppl. 254, 258 (M.D. Fla. 1982) *citing Gentry - Futch v. Gentry*, 90 Fla. 595, 106 So. 473, 477-478 (Fla. 1925).

[45] §720.306 (2), F.S.

[46] §720.306 (9), F.S.

The association may employ any form of voting process permitted by the governing documents, and, unless otherwise prohibited by the documents, members of the association may vote by proxy.[47] If ballots are used in the election process, the balloting, by its parliamentary nature, is a secret voting procedure.[48]

Any election dispute between a member and the association must be submitted by petition to mandatory binding arbitration with the Division of Florida Land Sales, Condominiums and Mobile Homes.[49] The petition must set forth the nature of the dispute, and it must be resolved by the arbitrator on an expedited basis under the procedural rules of the Division.[50]

2.11 Decorum. Decorum for a successful meeting is built on mutual respect between the membership and the presiding officer of the meeting.[51] Members wishing to speak should be presented through the chairman of the meeting.[52] Members wishing to obtain the floor for any purpose should do so properly by seeking the recognition of the presiding officer. Once a member assumes the floor, the rules of debate should be obeyed, and all comments should be confined to the question before the meet-

---

[47] §720.306 (8), F.S.

[48] *Robert's Rules of Order Newly Revised* (1990), §44; *Fletcher's Cyclopedia on Corporations, Corporate Meetings and Elections*, §2017.

[49] §720.306 (9), F.S.

[50] §§718.1255 (4) and (5), F.S.

[51] "Aside from express regulations, all that is necessary is that the meeting be conducted by the proper persons, with fairness and good faith towards all who are entitled to take part, and in such a way as to enable them to express their vote upon questions coming before the meeting." *Fletcher's Cyclopedia on Corporations, Corporate Meetings and Elections*, §2012.

[52] "The presiding officer of a ... meeting has no authority to defeat the will of the majority by arbitrary rulings, since the will of the majority is binding on him when legally expressed. Thus, a presiding officer cannot wrongfully declare the result of a vote or arbitrarily refuse to entertain or put motions." 18A *Am Jur.* 2d, Corporations, §991.

ing. Comments and statements relating to personal motives and to personalities should not be made and may be ruled out of order by the presiding officer.[53]

Proper decorum at a meeting is no more than the exercise of common courtesy and maintaining respect for the rights of others. To ensure that decorum is maintained, the presiding officer of the meeting should guide members through the proper order of business. The presiding officer must require that the rules be followed at all times. At the same time, the chairman must be both flexible and patient with members who are unfamiliar with the formal rules of parliamentary procedure.[54] The chairman should not permit conduct which is disruptive, tedious or dilatory.

2.12 Speaking at Membership Meetings. It is the right of all association members to speak at any meeting of the membership with reference to all items open for discussion or included on the meeting agenda. The board of directors of the association may adopt reasonable rules governing the frequency, duration, and manner of member statements, but the rules must be in writing and must permit a member to speak for at least three (3) minutes on any item. The association rules may additionally require that an owner submit a written request to speak prior to the meeting.[55]

2.13 Recording and Taping Membership Meetings. Any parcel owner may tape-record or videotape meetings of the association membership. The right to record meetings may be subject to restrictions imposed by the board of directors, provided that the restrictions are reasonable and have been adopted as

---

[53] *Robert's Rules of Order Newly Revised* (1990), §42.
[54] *Id.*
[55] §720.306 (6), F.S.

rules of the homeowners association by the board of directors.[56] Examples of such reasonable rules would include restrictions requiring prior notice by the member desiring to make a recording, restrictions requiring installation of the recording equipment prior to the commencement of the meeting and restrictions on recording equipment that produce distracting sound or light emissions.

2.14 Adjournment to a Different Time. It is permissible to adjourn a membership meeting for the purpose of reconvening to conclude the business of the meeting at a different time and place. Unless the association bylaws require otherwise, the adjournment of a meeting to a different date, time and place must be announced at the meeting before an adjournment is taken.[57] Otherwise, notice for the reconvened portion of the meeting must be posted in a conspicuous place in the community at least forty-eight (48) hours in advance of the meeting, or, in the alternative, notice must be mailed or delivered to each member at the last known address seven (7) days before the reconvened meeting.[58]

Any business that might have been transacted on the original date of the membership meeting may be transacted when the meeting is reconvened.[59] Special attention must be given to the proxies that have been returned for the meeting, however, since the proxies expire ninety (90) days after the date of the meeting for which they were originally given.[60]

---

[56] §720.306 (10), F.S.

[57] §720.306 (7), F.S.

[58] §720.306 (7) and §720.303 (2), F.S. For communities with more than one hundred (100) members, the bylaws may provide for a reasonable alternative to posting or mailing of notice. §720.303 (2), F.S.

[59] §720.306 (7), F.S.

[60] §720.306 (8), F.S.

2.15 Smoking and the "Clean Indoor Air Act." In November of 2002, Floridians approved a constitutional amendment banning smoking of all tobacco products in enclosed indoor locations where work is performed.[61] The definition of "work" includes all indoor meetings of the board of directors, committees of the board, and meetings of the membership, and accordingly, no smoking is permitted at these meetings. The definition is also sufficiently broad to include all indoor common areas of the community where work or service is performed by an officer, director, manager, employee, contractor or volunteer, and the simple cleaning or maintenance of the enclosed common areas is sufficient to impose a ban on smoking within these areas.[62]

It is the responsibility of the board of directors to establish appropriate policies prohibiting smoking in enclosed indoor workplaces within the community, and policies may include the posting of "no smoking" signs as the board deems appropriate.[63] Persons violating the Clean Indoor Air Act are subject to a $100.00 fine for the first occurrence and a $500.00 fine for each subsequent occurrence.[64]

---

[61] §2, Article X, Constitution of Florida.

[62] §386.203 (5) and (12), F.S.

[63] §386.206 (2), F.S.

[64] §386.208, F.S.

3

Board of Directors
and Meetings of the Board

3.1 General. The operation and management of the community's affairs are vested in the homeowners association. The board of directors is responsible for carrying out the duties and responsibilities of the homeowners association.[1] To the extent that the association has control of the affairs and the property of the community, the board of directors has the responsibility to implement that authority.[2]

The board of directors must consist of three (3) or more individuals with the actual number fixed in accordance with the articles of incorporation.[3] Directors will serve for a term of one (1) year unless the articles of incorporation or the bylaws of the homeowners association provide for different terms of office.[4] Unless the articles of incorporation or the bylaws of the association provide to the contrary, the board of directors may fix the compensation of directors.[5]

The authority of the board of directors is comprehensive and includes all of the powers and duties enumerated in Chapter 617 of the Florida Statutes (Florida Not For Profit Corporation Act), as long as the powers are not inconsistent with the provisions of the documents governing the community and the homeowners association.[6]

3.2 Election and Selection. The articles of incorporation or the bylaws of the homeowners association must provide the manner for the selection and the election of the members of the board of directors.[7] Generally, there are two methods for select-

---

[1] §617.01401(2), F.S.
[2] §617.0801, F.S.
[3] §617.0803, F.S.
[4] §617.0803 (3) and §617.0806, F.S.
[5] §617.08101, F.S.
[6] §720.303 (1) and §617.0302, F.S.
[7] §720.306 (9) and §617.0803 (3), F.S.

ing members to serve on the board. The first, and most common, is by election to the board by members of the association at an annual or special meeting.[8] (See 2.10.) The second method of selection is by appointment to the board of directors. The appointment may occur by the developer if the developer is still entitled to representation[9] or it may be by the remaining members of the board of directors when a vacancy on the board occurs between meetings of the membership.

When a vacancy arises on the board of directors between meetings of the membership, the remaining board members may select a new member by appointment. Vacancies on the board may be filled by the remaining board members even if the remaining members are less than a majority of the full board of directors.[10] The term of a board member appointed to fill a vacancy will continue for the unexpired term of his or her predecessor in office. At the expiration of the term, a replacement member to the board can be elected by the membership.[11]

3.3 Failure to Fill Board Vacancies. If a homeowners association fails to fill vacancies on the board of directors sufficient to constitute a quorum, any member of the association may apply to the circuit court for the appointment of a receiver to manage the affairs of the association. At least thirty (30) days before applying to the court, the member must advise the association and its other members of the intended action by posting notice in a conspicuous place in the community and by mailing notice to the association by certified or registered mail. If the association fails to fill a sufficient number of vacancies within thirty (30) days so that a quorum of the board can be assembled, the member may proceed with the petition in circuit court.[12]

---

8   §720.306 (2), F.S.
9   §720.307 (1) and (2), F.S.
10 §617.0809 (1), F.S.
11 §617.0809 (2), F.S.
12 §720.305 (3), F.S.

When a receiver is appointed by the court, the homeowners association is responsible for the salary of the receiver, court costs and attorney's fees, and all other costs of the receivership. The receiver possesses all of the powers and duties of a duly constituted board of directors and serves until the homeowners association fills vacancies on the board sufficient to constitute a quorum.[13]

3.4   The Developer and Transition of Control. The provisions of the statute specifically governing homeowners associations do not mandate any schedule for transition of control of the board of directors from the developer to the members for homeowners associations created prior to June 15, 1995.[14] For such associations, the developer appoints the first complete board of directors of the association, and the developer will continue to control the board under the terms prescribed by the articles of incorporation, bylaws and other governing documents.[15]

For homeowners associations created after June 15, 1995, the law provides a schedule of transition from developer control to control by members other than the developer. Under the statutory schedule, the members are entitled to elect at least a majority of the members of the board of directors of the association three (3) months after ninety (90) percent of the parcels in all phases of the community to be operated by the homeowners association have been conveyed to members of the association.[16] A different percentage may apply if it is required in order

---

[13]   *Id.*

[14]   §720.307 (3), F.S. The exemption also extends to a homeowners association, no matter when created, if it is in a community that is included in an effective development-of-regional-impact development order that is in effect on or before June 15, 1995.

[15]   §720.302 (2) and §617.0803 (3), F.S.

[16]   §720.307 (1) (a) and (c), F.S. "Members other than the developer" do not include builders, contractors or others who purchase a parcel for purposes of constructing improvements on the property for resale.

to comply with the requirements of any governmentally chartered entity with regard to the mortgage financing of parcels in the community, provided that this alternative transition requirement is set out in the governing documents of the community.[17]

Within 90 days of the time that the owners are entitled to elect at least a majority of the board of directors of the association, the developer must, at the developer's expense, deliver the books and records of the association to the new board. The required records include the original community documents, the corporate minute book and financial records of the association, insurance policies and other contracts of the association, resignations of the developer-directors, any governmental permits issued to the association, a list of the names and addresses (with telephone numbers) of all contractors and employees of the association, and control of all funds of the association and other property. The documents also include any warranties in effect at the time of transition, a roster of the current homeowners and their addresses, and all other written records of the association.[18]

During the time the board of directors is controlled by the developer, the operational procedures, record keeping and the election and voting requirements specified by statute are applicable to the homeowners association.[19] The provisions in the law governing association operations do not, however, impair the rights of the developer to complete the community as contemplated.[20]

3.5 Eligibility. The articles of incorporation or bylaws of the homeowners association will specify and provide the eligibility

---

[17] §720.307 (1) (b), F.S.
[18] §720.303 (4), F.S.
[19] §720.303 and §720.306, F.S.
[20] §720.302 (2), F.S.

requirements for the members of the board of directors. Florida's law does not require individual board members to be members of the association or residents of the state unless the articles of incorporation or bylaws impose these qualifications.[21] The law does, however, declare that all members of the association are eligible to serve as a member of the board of directors, and any member may nominate himself or herself as a candidate for the board of directors at the meeting of members where the election is to be held.[22]

When eligibility is limited to ownership and a parcel is owned jointly, each of the owners is qualified to serve on the board even though only one of the owners may be designated to exercise the parcel's voting rights. When a parcel is owned by a corporation or another type of artificial person such as a partnership or trust, determining the eligibility for a representative of the parcel to serve on the board of directors presents a unique dilemma. If the bylaws permit, the designated voting representative of the corporation may be eligible for the board. If eligibility is contingent upon association membership, then the parcel may be effectively excluded from offering a candidate for the board since a corporation cannot sit as a member of the board of directors.[23]

An exception to this eligibility standard is made when the lot or parcel is owned by a trust. If a lot is owned by a trust and the grantors or beneficiaries of the trust occupy the parcel, then the occupants are considered members of the association and are eligible for service on the board of directors.[24]

Membership in the homeowners association passes with ownership of a parcel.[25] When a parcel is sold, the membership

---

[21] §617.0802, F.S.
[22] §720.306 (9), F.S.
[23] *Id.*
[24] §617.0802 (2), F.S.
[25] §720.301 (9) and (11), F.S.

in the homeowners association is also transferred to the new owner. When ownership is an eligibility requirement for service on the board, transfer of a parcel will terminate the eligibility of an individual to serve on the board of directors and create a vacancy on the board at the time of sale.

3.6   Resignation, Recall and Removal. A member of the board of directors may voluntarily resign at any time by delivery of his or her written notice of resignation to the board of directors, to its chairman or to the homeowners association.[26] The resignation is effective when the notice is delivered unless the notice specifies a later effective date. When the resignation is effective at a later date, the remaining directors may fill the pending vacancy before the effective date, provided the successor does not take office until the vacancy is effective.[27]

Any member of the board of directors may be recalled and removed with or without cause by a majority of the total voting interests eligible to elect the board member.[28] The recall may be by written agreement or by written ballot without a membership meeting, and the recall documentation must be served on the association by certified mail or by personal service.[29] When the recall documentation is received, the board of directors shall notice and hold a meeting within five (5) business days to certify the ballots or the recall agreement. Once the documentation is certified, the recall is effective immediately, and the director or directors recalled shall turn over any and all property of the association in their possession within five (5) working days of the certification by the board.[30]

If the recall procedures remove less than a majority of the

---

26   §617.0807 (1), F.S.
27   §617.0807 (2), F.S.
28   §720.303 (10) (b) 1, F.S.
29   *Id.*
30   §720.303 (10) (b) 2, F.S.

board of directors, the vacancy or vacancies created may be filled by an affirmative vote of the remaining directors. When the recall results in the removal of a majority or more of the board of directors, the vacancies shall be filled by the members voting in favor of the recall.[31] In such circumstances, the written recall agreement or recall ballots must list at least as many possible replacement directors as there are directors subject to recall, permitting the person executing the recall instrument or ballot to vote for the replacement of the directors subject to the recall.[32]

In the event that the board of directors determines to reject some or all of the recall votes and not to certify the recall, the board shall file a petition for binding arbitration for the resolution of the dispute with the Department of Business and Professional Regulation within five (5) days.[33] The minutes of the board meeting must identify the specific reason for rejecting a member's recall vote and the parcel number owned by the member whose vote is rejected.[34] The Department arbitrator is required to expedite consideration of the dispute and the matter is finalized when the final order of arbitration is issued.[35]

As an alternative recall procedure, when the community documents specifically permit, the association members may recall a board member or members by a vote at a membership meeting called by ten (10) percent of the voting interests of the association. After the membership vote approving the recall, the board is required to call a meeting with five (5) days to certify the results or proceed with arbitration.[36]

3.7   Fiduciary Relationship. The members of the board of

---

[31]   §720.303 (10) (e), F.S.

[32]   §720.303 (10) (b) 5 and §720.303 (10) (i), F.S.

[33]   §720.303 (10) (d), F.S.

[34]   §720.303 (10) (h), F.S.

[35]   §720.303 (10) (d), F.S.

[36]   §720.303 (10) (c), F.S.

directors and each officer of the homeowners association have a fiduciary relationship with the members of the association.[37] This fiduciary relationship imposes obligations of trust and confidence in favor of the association and its members. It requires each member of the board to act in good faith and in a manner he or she believes to be in the best interests of the members of the association. It means the board members must exercise the care and diligence of an ordinarily prudent person when acting for the community, and it requires each of them to act within the scope of their authority.[38]

Directors and officers of the association must devote enough time and effort to the performance of their duties to ensure that they are reasonably and faithfully carried out on behalf of the association. The fact that the homeowners association is a corporation not for profit, or that the members of the board are volunteers and unpaid, does not relieve them from the standards of trust and responsibility that the fiduciary relationship requires.[39]

3.8   Indemnification. When directors and officers of the homeowners association are properly carrying out their duties within the scope of responsibility assigned to them, they may be indemnified by the association and its members when claims or suits are brought against them for their actions. The right of indemnification does not, however, extend to members of the board of directors appointed by the developer,[40] and association funds may not be used by a developer to defend actions filed against the developer or directors appointed by the developer even when the proceedings concern the operations of the developer-controlled association.[41]

---

[37]   §720.303 (1), F.S.
[38]   §617.0830 (1), F.S.
[39]   §720.303 (1), F.S.
[40]   §617.0831, F.S.
[41]   §720.303 (8) (c), F.S.

In fulfilling their duties and responsibilities, board members and officers may utilize certain information provided by others when discharging duties on the association's behalf. Information, opinions and reports from officers and employees of the association whom the director believes to be reliable and competent may be relied upon, and the advice and opinions of legal counsel and other professionals may also be appropriately used.[42]

3.9   Meetings of the Board. Actions of the board of directors take place at meetings of the board. A meeting of the board of directors includes any gathering of a quorum of the members for the purpose of conducting homeowners association business. Meetings may be either a regular or special gathering, and they may be called by the chairman, the president or any other persons who are authorized to do so by the bylaws of the association.[43] Unless the bylaws place a restriction on the place of the meeting, it may be held wherever the board of directors finds it necessary. The place may include the offices of the association's attorney, accountant, or manager or another location deemed appropriate by the board.[44]

Unless prohibited by the articles of incorporation or bylaws, the board of directors may permit any or all directors to participate in a meeting by means of communication, such as by conference call, so long as all directors may simultaneously hear each other during the meeting. A director participating in a board meeting in this manner is considered to be present at the meeting.[45] A director is not permitted to vote by proxy or by secret ballot at board meetings, except that directors may vote by secret ballot when electing officers of the homeowners association.[46]

---

[42] §617.0830 (2), F.S.
[43] *See generally* §617.0820, §617.0824 (3), and §720.303 (2), F.S.
[44] §617.0820 (1), F.S.
[45] §617.0820 (4), F.S.
[46] §720.303 (2), F.S.

A quorum of the board of directors consists of a majority of the members of the board established in the articles of incorporation or the bylaws.[47] When a quorum is present, the affirmative vote of a majority of the directors present is an act of the board unless the articles or bylaws require the vote of a greater number of directors.[48] A director who is present when an action is taken is deemed to have agreed with the action unless he or she votes against the action or affirmatively abstains or objects at the beginning of the meeting to holding the meeting or transacting specified affairs at the meeting.[49] The minutes of the meeting should reflect the vote of each board member on each action taken at the meeting.

Florida's corporate law permits the board of directors to take action without a meeting if all of the board members consent to the action in writing unless the articles of incorporation or bylaws provide otherwise. The written consent will have the same effect as if a unanimous vote had been taken at a meeting. An action taken without a meeting of the board becomes effective when the last director signs the consent unless the consent specifies a different effective date.[50]

3.10 Notice to Board Members. There are two types of notice which must be given before a proper meeting of the board of directors of a homeowners association can be held. The first is for the individual members of the board, and the second is for the general association membership. The notice to members of the board of directors can be made by first-class mail, by personal delivery, by telegram or electronic transmission, and notice must be given at least two (2) days prior to the meeting itself. The provisions of the association's bylaws may pro-

---

47 §617.0824 (1), F.S. The articles of incorporation or the bylaws of the association may provide for a quorum of less than a majority but no fewer than one-third of the prescribed number of directors.

48 §617.0824 (3), F.S.

49 §720.303 (3) and §617.0824 (4), F.S.

50 §617.0821, F.S.

vide for different notice requirements and for longer or shorter periods of time.[51] (See 6.11.)

Notice to board members for regular meetings of the board may be dispensed with unless notice is required by the articles of incorporation or bylaws,[52] and notice may be waived by board members who sign a waiver of notice either before or after the meeting.[53]

3.11 Notice to Association Members. All board meetings of the association must be open to the members of the homeowners association except for meetings between the board and its attorney with respect to proposed or pending litigation where the contents of the discussion would be governed by the attorney-client privilege. Accordingly, the members of the association are entitled to notice of the meetings of the board.[54] The requirement for open meetings extends not only to meetings of the board but to all committees of the board and executive councils which are carrying out a portion of the association's responsibilities.[55]

The law provides alternative methods for providing notice to the association membership. Notice of most board meetings must be conspicuously posted on the association property at least forty-eight (48) hours in advance of each meeting, except in an emergency. In the alternative, if notice is not posted, it must be mailed, electronically transmitted or delivered to each member of the association at least seven (7) days before the meeting, except in an emergency. If the community is served by a closed-circuit television system, the notice may be given by broadcasting the notice at least four (4) times every broadcast

---

[51] §617.0822 (2), F.S.
[52] §617.0822 (1), F.S.
[53] §617.0823, F.S.
[54] §720.303 (2) (a), F.S.
[55] *Id.*

hour of each day that a posted notice is otherwise required. In communities where the homeowners association has more than one hundred (100) members, the bylaws of the association may provide a reasonable alternative to the general notice requirements of posting or mailing of the notice.[56]

Special notice requirements apply when a board meeting is scheduled to consider assessments against parcels in the community or when changes in the rules and regulations that govern the use of parcels in the community will be considered. The written notice for board meetings scheduled to consider these topics must be provided to members at least fourteen (14) days prior to the meeting, and when an assessment it to be considered, the notice must so state and describe the nature of the assessment. When changes to the rules will be considered, the notice must contain a statement that the board is considering changes to the rules and regulations.[57]

3.12 Membership Participation. Members of the homeowners association have the right to attend all meetings of the board of directors and also have the right to speak before the board on any matter that has been placed on the meeting agenda by petition.[58] To place an item of business on the agenda of the board, twenty (20) percent or more of the total voting interests of the association must file a petition with the board making the request.

Each member of the association shall have the right to speak for at least three (3) minutes on each matter placed on the agenda by petition, provided that the member signs the sign-up sheet, if one is provided, or submits a written request to speak

---

[56] §720.303 (2) (c) 1, F.S.
[57] §720.303 (2) (c) 2, F.S.
[58] §720.303 (2) (b), F.S.

prior to the meeting. The board of directors is required to give all members fourteen (14) days notice of the meeting at which the petitioned item or items will be addressed, but the board is not obligated to take any other action requested by the petition.[59]

While membership participation is not required at board meetings except by petition, many homeowners associations do set aside a specific part of the agenda so that individual members can make presentations to the board of directors. The association is permitted to adopt written rules permitting members to speak and governing the frequency and duration of the participation by members at board meetings.[60] Maintaining a regular portion of the agenda for membership comment helps to diffuse controversy and problems and permits the board of directors to have regular and orderly communications from members of the association. When considering the rules for member participation, the board should also consider how it can best be handled in an orderly fashion. A specific part of the agenda for member participation is, in most cases, a more preferable alternative to continuous member involvement throughout the full agenda of the board meeting.

Members are permitted to tape-record or videotape meetings of the board of directors, although the board may adopt reasonable rules to govern the taping.[61] (See 2.13.) Finally, notwithstanding other provisions of law, the requirement that board meetings be open to the members is inapplicable to meetings between the board and the association's attorney concerning pending or threatened litigation and with respect to meetings of the board held for the purpose of discussing personnel matters.[62]

---

[59] §720.303 (2) (d), F.S.

[60] §720.303 (2) (b), F.S.

[61] §720.306 (10), F.S.

[62] §720.303 (2) (b), F.S.

3.13 Committees. The board of directors, in addition to selecting the officers of the homeowners association, may also designate an executive committee and other committees unless prohibited by the articles of incorporation or the bylaws.[63] The committees are created by resolution of the board of directors, and each committee exercising some authority of the board of directors must include two or more members of the board.[64]

Committees authorized to spend association funds or committees vested with the power to approve architectural decisions in the community must follow the same notice, quorum and voting requirements imposed upon the board of directors of the association. Meetings of these committees are open to members of the association, and committee members are not permitted to vote by proxy or by secret ballot.[65]

Advisory committees also have a place within the organization of the homeowners association. They are not authorized by the community documents or by statute to carry out functions for the association or to exercise any authority on behalf of the board of directors.[66] Such advisory committees help analyze problems, review facts and gather information and alternatives. Their conclusions and recommendations are reported to the board of directors or to the officer of the homeowners association creating the advisory committee. As with other committees, the notice, quorum and voting requirements imposed by statute apply to advisory committees.[67]

---

[63] §617.0825 (1), F.S.

[64] §617.0825 (3), F.S.

[65] §720.303 (2) (c) 3, F.S.

[66] §617.0825 (1), F.S.

[67] §720.303 (2) (c) 3 , F.S.

4

Officers

4.1 General. The homeowners association can only carry out acts through its officers and agents. The board of directors makes the policies for the association, but the officers and agents carry out these policies and administrative functions for the community.[1] Some of the officers are merely clerical or ministerial while others carry out substantive functions based on the policies established by the board. All of the officers of the homeowners association have a fiduciary relationship to the members of the association. The officers have an affirmative obligation to act with utmost good faith towards the association and cannot deal in the funds or the property of the association to their own advantage.[2]

Each homeowners association shall have such officers as are described in the articles of incorporation or bylaws. The officers shall serve for the terms prescribed in the association documents, and, if terms are not established, the officers shall be appointed by the board of directors annually.[3] The officers most commonly described by the association documents are a president, secretary, treasurer and one or more vice presidents. Collectively, the officers will perform the duties established in the bylaws and carry out the management responsibilities of the homeowners association under the policies approved by the board of directors.[4]

4.2 Election of Officers. The officers of the homeowners association are elected, or appointed, by the board of directors. They are not elected by the membership of the association unless the bylaws of the association specifically require a membership vote for a particular office.[5] The officers are elected by a majority vote of the board of directors,[6] and the board is per-

---

[1] §617.0841, F.S.
[2] §720.303 (1), F.S.
[3] §617.0840 (1), F.S.
[4] §617.0841, F.S.
[5] §617.0840 (1), F.S.
[6] §617.0824 (3), F.S.

mitted to conduct the election for officers by secret ballot.[7] When the bylaws or the board of directors allow, any duly appointed or elected officer of the homeowners association may appoint one or more officers or assistant officers.[8] (See 4.8.)

4.3   President. The president of the homeowners association is traditionally vested with all the powers generally given to the chief executive officer of a corporation.[9] While specific bylaw provisions may vary the president's duties, it is generally presumed that he or she will preside at all meetings of the board of directors and the membership.[10] The president will execute contracts approved by the board and other documents in the name of the association as its agent. When signing documents, the president should indicate the capacity in which he or she is signing to avoid any personal liability since the president's signature, under most circumstances, will bind the homeowners association under the doctrine of inherent powers.[11]

The president also assumes general charge of the day-to-day administration of the association and has the authority to authorize specific actions in furtherance of the board's policies. As chief executive officer, the president serves as spokesperson for the board of directors in most matters relating to general association business.[12] Like all officers of the association, the president has an affirmative duty to carry out the responsibilities of the office in the best interests of the association. The president serves at the will of the board of directors and can be

---

[7] §720.303 (2) (c) 3, F.S.

[8] §617.0840 (2), F.S.

[9] *Pan-American Construction Co. v. Searcy*, 84 So.2d 540 (Fla. 1955); 18B *Am. Jur.* 2d, Corporations, §1534.

[10] *Robert's Rules of Order Newly Revised* (1990), §46.

[11] *Snead v. United States Trucking Corp.*, 380 So.2d 1075, 1078 (Fla. 1st DCA 1980); *Pan-American Construction Corp. v. Searcy, supra* note 9.

[12] 18B *Am. Jur.* 2d, Corporations, §1534.

removed with or without cause at any time by majority vote of the full board.[13]

The president cannot, without specific board approval, borrow funds in the name of the association or otherwise act beyond the scope of the authority established by the homeowners association documents and board of directors.[14] The president does have the inherent authority to appoint committees to advise him and to advise the board. The president also has the authority to appoint certain officers to assist him with his duties such as vote tellers, inspectors of elections, sergeants at arms and a temporary secretary or recorder unless the bylaws otherwise make some provision for selection of these positions.[15]

4.4 Secretary. The bylaws or the board of directors are required to delegate to one of the officers responsibility for preparing notice for all meetings of the board and the membership and authenticating the records of the association.[16] Customarily, such responsibilities are delegated to the secretary. The position of secretary is not simply a clerical position, however. In many cases, the secretary will not actually keep the minutes of the meetings but will be responsible for obtaining someone who will do so as a recorder or assistant secretary. As the custodian of the minutes and the other official records of the association, the secretary is responsible for ensuring access to those records by members and their authorized representatives.[17] (See 6.6.)

---

[13] §617.0842 (2), F.S.; *Frank v. Anthony*, 107 So.2d 136 (Fla. 2d DCA 1958).

[14] *See Wenger v. Breakwater Homeowners' Ass'n*, 423 So.2d 619 (Fla. 4th DCA 1982), applying the general corporate law principle that a corporation's powers are limited to those expressed in the articles of incorporation and those implied powers necessary to perform the authorized functions of the association.

[15] 18B *Am. Jur.* 2d, Corporations, §1534; *Fletcher's Cyclopedia on Corporations*, Private Corporations, §533.

[16] §617.0840 (3), F.S.

[17] §720.303 (3) and (4), F.S.

The homeowners association is authorized to adopt and use a "corporate seal."[18] When the secretary has been delegated the responsibility for authenticating records of the homeowners association, the verification customarily occurs by affixing a signature and placing the corporate seal on the appropriate document. By example, when the signature of the president binds the corporation, and the secretary, as custodian of the seal, verifies the president's authority, the secretary does so by signing or attesting to the president's signature and placing the corporate seal on the appropriate document.

4.5   Treasurer. The treasurer is traditionally the custodian of the funds, securities and financial records of the association. When the association has a manager or other employee that actually handles the funds, then the treasurer's duties will include overseeing the appropriate employees to ensure that the financial records and reports are properly kept and maintained. Unless the bylaws otherwise specify, the treasurer is responsible for coordinating the development of the proposed annual budget and for preparing and giving the annual financial report.[19] (See 5.8.)

The treasurer does not have the authority to bind the association or the board of directors when dealing with third parties unless the board has provided express authority for the treasurer to do so.[20] As with the association's secretary, the treasurer does not have to actually perform the day-to-day record-keeping functions of the association, but the treasurer will ultimately be responsible to make sure that the financial records of the homeowners association have been maintained properly in accordance with good accounting practices.

---

[18] §617.0302 (3), F.S.; the seal must always contain the words "corporation not for profit." *Id.*

[19] *Fletcher's Cyclopedia on Corporations*, Private Corporations, §654; 18B *Am. Jur.* 2d, Corporations, §1538.

[20] *Ideal Foods, Inc. v. Action Leasing Corp.*, 413 So. 2d 416, 417 (Fla. 5th DCA 1982).

4.6   Vice President. The vice president of the homeowners association is vested with all of the powers which are required to perform the duties of the association president in the absence of the president.[21] The vice president does not automatically possess inherent powers to act in the capacity of chief executive and may act for the president only when the president is actually absent or otherwise unable to act.[22] The vice president may assume such additional duties as are defined or assigned by the board of directors of the association.[23]

In many communities, the vice president will be assigned specific areas of responsibility which may include overseeing the care and maintenance of the grounds and buildings, the recreational properties or other association properties. The vice president may also be designated to serve as the executive director or the employee manager for the association. Each of these duties must be specifically conveyed by the board of directors upon the vice president, and the scope of this authority and responsibility should be defined in writing and placed in the minutes or in the bylaws of the homeowners association.

4.7   Registered Agent and Office. The registered agent is a ministerial officer of the homeowners association, and it is an officer that is required of all corporations in Florida.[24] In addition to naming a registered agent, each homeowners association must also maintain a registered office for the corporation, although it does not need to be the same as the association's place of business.[25] The registered agent receives all formal service of legal papers on behalf of the association, including all lawsuits.

---

[21]   18B *Am. Jur.* 2d, Corporations, §1537; *Fletcher's Cyclopedia on Corporations*, Private Corporations, §627.

[22]   *Pan-American Construction Co. v. Searcy, supra* note 9; *see also Robert's Rules of Order Newly Revised* (1990), §46.

[23]   §617.0841, F.S.

[24]   §617.0501 (1) (a), F.S.

[25]   §617.0501 (1) (b), F.S.

The registered agent is an important link for the homeowners association since many formal and important communications will be received by this association officer.[26] When these communications or documents are received, they must be brought immediately to the attention of the board of directors. The registered agent must be aware of the responsibilities of the office, and the board of directors may desire to assign this responsibility to a member of the current board or to the association's legal counsel.

The name of the registered agent and the street address of the registered office can be changed by the board of directors at any time by simply filing written notice with the Division of Corporations. The address for the registered office of the association must be a street address. A post office box is not acceptable. The new registered agent must sign the change in designation, acknowledging and accepting the responsibilities of the position.[27]

4.8   Other Officers. The homeowners association shall have such other officers as are provided for in the articles of incorporation, and such officers and assistant officers as may be authorized by the association bylaws or the board of directors.[28] Other officers may include an assistant secretary, additional vice presidents or other positions which will serve merely as agents to carry out specific association responsibilities. These other officers will help divide the responsibilities of the association into manageable categories, and each office can be assigned specific authority by the board of directors to carry out the assigned duties and responsibilities.[29]

---

[26] §607.0505, F.S.
[27] §617.0502, F.S.
[28] §617.0840 (1) and (2), F.S.
[29] §617.0841, F.S.

The responsibilities of supplemental association officers may include the authority to sign liens, demand letters, and checks for the association. They may include the authority to manage the day-to-day maintenance responsibilities for the association or other specific activities sanctioned by the board.[30] Custom allows third parties to rely on agents and officers of the association. A commitment made in the normal course of business by agents and officers may bind the association. (See 4.9.) When creating additional offices, the board should specify, in writing, the scope of authority for the office and the specific duties and responsibilities of the officer. The limits imposed upon the officer's authority should also be expressed.

4.9 Scope of Authority. The officers and agents of the homeowners association must carry out their duties within the scope of authority conferred upon the office.[31] The relationship between an officer and the association is that of principal and agent.[32] When the officer is acting on the homeowners association's behalf and within the scope of his or her authority, the association is bound by the acts of the officer or agent.[33] Individual association members or members of the public at large acting in good faith may rely on the "real" or "apparent" authority of an officer to bind the homeowners association.[34]

The "real" authority of an association officer is that which is expressly set out in the association's bylaws or in resolutions of the board of directors and which is actually known

---

[30] *Id.*

[31] *See B & J Holding Corp. v. Miller*, 353 So.2d 141, 143 (Fla. 3d DCA 1977).

[32] *Thomkin Corp. v. Miller*, 24 So.2d 48 (Fla. 1945).

[33] §617.0841, F.S.; *see also Stiles v. Gordon Land Co.*, 44 So.2d 417 (Fla. 1950) *citing Thomkin Corp. v. Miller, supra* note 32; *see also Edward J. Gerrits, Inc. v. McKinney*, 410 So.2d 542, 545 (Fla. 1st DCA 1982).

[34] *Id.*

to the party dealing with the officer.[35] The "apparent" authority of an officer is grounded in the doctrine of estoppel.[36] It arises when the homeowners association allows or causes others to believe the officer has such authority through its actions or representations.[37] It may exist or arise from the very nature of the office itself.[38] Through an officer's authority, real or apparent, the association makes its financial commitments, enters into contracts for service and otherwise carries on the business of the association.[39]

4.10 Resignation and Removal. Any officer of the homeowners association may resign at any time by delivering his or her written resignation to the association. The resignation is effective when the notice is delivered by the officer unless the notice specifies a later effective date. When the resignation is effective at a later date, the vacant office may be filled before the effective date of the resignation provided the successor does not take office until the vacancy is effective.[40]

An officer of the association may be removed by the board of directors at any time with or without cause. An officer or assistant officer appointed by another officer may likewise be removed at any time with or without cause by the officer of the homeowners association who made the appointment.[41]

---

[35]   18 B. *Am. Jur.* 2d, Corporations, §1521.

[36]   "Its (the doctrine of estoppel) three primary elements are: (1) representation by the principal, (2) reliance upon that representation by a third person, and (3) a change of position by the third person in reliance upon such representation." *Ideal Foods, Inc. v. Action Leasing Corp.*, 413 So.2d 416, 418 (Fla. 5th DCA 1982) *citing Stiles v. Gordon Land Co.*, *supra* note 33.

[37]   *Taco Bell of California v. Zappone*, 324 So.2d 121, 123-124 (Fla. 2d DCA 1975).

[38]   *Pan-American Construction Co. v. Searcy, supra* note 9.

[39]   *Dade County Dairies, Inc. v. Projected Planning Co.*, 158 So.2d 565 (Fla. 3d DCA 1963); *see also* 18B *Am. Jur.* 2d, Corporations, §1519 and §1521.

[40]   §617.0842 (1), F.S.

[41]   §617.0842 (2), F.S.

5

Budget and Finances

5.1   General. Each homeowners association is required to keep its financial records according to generally accepted accounting principles.[1] Key among these financial records is the financial plan that sets forth the proposed expenditure of funds for the maintenance of the properties under the association's control and for the management and operation of the association itself. The financial plan, or budget, is the foundation document for the association's financial operation and stability. It provides a preview of the coming year's expenses, and it provides a benchmark by which the previous year's expenditures can be judged and evaluated.

The budget must be prepared annually by the community for a twelve-month period.[2] Once adopted, it becomes the basis for allocating the individual assessment shares among each of the members of the homeowners association. The manner for allocating shares among the members of the association will be established by the community documents. Upon adoption of the budget, the required annual assessment or amenity fee of each parcel owner in the community is also simultaneously set, and the owner becomes obligated to pay the association the sums due for the operation of the community.[3] Notice of any meeting of the board of directors in which assessments against parcels are to be established, including assessments to fund the annual budget, must be specially prepared to advise parcel owners concerning the nature of the assessments.[4] (See 5.6.)

5.2   Recurring Operations. The budget for the homeowners association must provide an accurate, itemized and detailed listing of all the expenses that the community reasonably believes will be incurred during the coming fiscal year. The main cate-

---

[1]   §720.303 (4) (j), F.S.
[2]   §720.303 (8), F.S.
[3]   §720.301 (11) (b), F.S.
[4]   §720.303 (2) (c) 2, F.S.

gories or components of the budget will govern the regular and ongoing operations of the homeowners association. These operations categories will deal with the everyday, recurring expenditures of the community, and they should identify each proposed category of expense separately, from administration to management, and from taxes to insurance.[5]

The expenses for general operations should be listed by account and classification, and they should be set out to show the total estimated monthly and annual expenditures for each classification. It is helpful to have the categories coded with a numbering system or other identifying subtitle so that actual expenditures through the course of the fiscal year can be allocated to the appropriate category or account.

5.3 Capital Expenses and Deferred Maintenance. In many communities, it is prudent to have a separate portion of the budget set aside that creates a surplus for capital expenditures and deferred maintenance. These "reserve" categories of the budget are for items of expense that do not occur on a regular basis, and their purpose is to provide funds for the longer-term needs of the homeowners association which involve major capital repairs or replacements to the homeowners association property. The reserve categories may include funds for roadways and repaving or for capital repairs to the community recreation building and other types of shared facilities. The reserve categories in the budget are designed to ensure that funds will be available when the repairs or replacements are needed without the necessity of a large special assessment against individual members of the homeowners association. These surplus

---

5   §720.303 (6), F.S.

reserve funds must be separately reflected in the association's budget.[6]

When preparing the reserve categories, the board of directors should attempt to establish a formula that will take into consideration the estimated useful life of the asset and the amount of money that will be required to make the repair or replacement when it is actually needed. The surplus funds that are collected in the current fiscal year can be placed in a separate interest bearing account until the need arises for the use of the funds. The basis or formula for establishing the reserve amounts should be stated as a part of the budget as a footnote so the information will be available for review by members of the association.[7]

5.4 Recreational Amenities. The recreational amenities serving the community may be owned by the association, the developer or another person. Notwithstanding their ownership, however, special treatment of the fees and charges for the recreational amenities is required under the law governing homeowners associations. The budget for the association is required to set out separately all fees and charges for recreational amenities no matter who retains ownership of the property.[8] In corresponding fashion, the annual financial report to the members must set out the actual receipts and expenditures for the recreational amenities.[9]

When parcel owners are required to pay maintenance or amenity fees directly to the developer or to another owner of recreational facilities or other properties, the owner of the facilities is required to provide a complete financial report of the

---

[6] §720.303 (6), F.S. The budget must reflect the estimated surplus anticipated at the end of the fiscal year.

[7] §720.303 (4) (j), F.S. The financial records of the association must be kept according to good accounting practices.

[8] §720.303 (6), F.S.

[9] §720.303 (7) (b), F.S.

actual, total receipts of the fees received from the parcel owners.[10] The report must be provided within sixty (60) days following the end of each fiscal year, and it may be given by mail to each parcel owner, by publishing it in a publication regularly distributed within the community or by posting it in prominent locations within the community.[11]

5.5 Developing the Proposed Budget. The "proposed budget" is the preliminary draft of the homeowners association's financial plan, and it is offered by the board or other association officer for formal adoption as the budget. The development of the proposed budget may be by the association's treasurer, a financial committee, the community's management company or by the board of directors itself.

The board should bring as much expertise as possible to the development of the proposed budget. The records of each homeowners association must include an accurate record of previous expenditures so that the proposed budget can be based on the association's financial history and the experience of the previous year's expenditures.[12] New anticipated expenses can be estimated from comparisons in the marketplace or from the experience of other homeowners associations. Each classification should be based upon realistic estimates and should be set forth in sufficient detail so that each category can be understood and evaluated by the members of the association and by the board of directors.

5.6 Funding the Budget. To fund the homeowners association's budget, the board of directors, in almost all circumstances, is granted authority to assess individual property own-

---

10 Any amounts paid to the homeowners association, to local governmental entities and special taxing districts do not need to be included in the report. §689.265, F.S.

11 §689.265, F.S.

12 *See* §720.303 (4) (j) 1. and 3., F.S.

ers for their share of the community's funding requirements.[13] The recorded declaration of covenants and the other governing documents of the association must be consulted to determine the basis for the assessment allocation.[14] The assessments must be allocated based upon the members' proportional shares as described in the governing documents, and it is permissible for the documents to provide for different shares among classes of parcel owners.[15]

In the unlikely event that no specific allocation is made in the community's documents, then the responsibility for funding the budget should be spread equally among the parcels of property represented in the homeowners association. For communities created after October 1, 1995, the governing documents are required to describe the manner in which expenses are shared by the members, and they must specify the proportional shares for which each member is responsible.[16]

Notice of the board of directors meeting where assessments are to be established must contain a specific statement that assessments will be considered and a statement concerning the nature of the assessments. The meeting notice must be mailed, delivered or electronically transmitted to each member of the homeowners association and posted in a conspicuous place on the association property at least fourteen (14) days before the meeting.[17] (See 3.11.)

When the amount of the annual assessment has been determined for each member, the board of directors is then required to establish a payment schedule for the owners. In many cases, the payment schedule will be set in the bylaws or in the covenants governing the association. If a schedule is not

---

[13] §720.301 (1), F.S.; *see Wood v. McElvey*, 296 So.2d 102 (Fla. 2d DCA 1974).

[14] *See Bessemer v. Gersten*, 381 So.2d 1344 (Fla. 1980).

[15] §720.308, F.S.

[16] *Id.*

[17] §720.303 (2) (b) 2, F.S.

set by the community documents, the board must, by resolution, determine whether the assessment will be paid in full or be divided into monthly or quarterly installments. The board of directors should require that payments be made in advance so that the funds are available to meet the current needs of the association as they arise.

When the annual budget has been approved, the board of directors must provide each member with a copy of the budget or written notice that a copy of the budget is available upon request at no charge to the member.[18] The association must also maintain a current account and a periodic statement of the account, designating the name of the member, the due date and amount of each assessment, the amount paid upon the account and the balance due from each member of the homeowners association.[19]

5.7   Assessment Responsibilities of the Developer. From the time of the creation of the community and until the sale of parcels to a purchaser, the developer is the owner of the parcels. As the parcel owner, the developer is liable for all assessments that come due unless the developer is excused from the payment of operating expenses and assessments by the declaration of covenants.

In order to be excused from payment, the developer must be obligated to pay any operating expenses incurred that exceed the assessments receivable from other members and any other income of the association. The developer's guarantee extends only for the period of time that the developer remains obligated to pay the excess operating expenses of the homeowners association.[20]

---

[18]   §720.303 (6), F.S.

[19]   §720.303 (4) (j) 2., F.S.

[20]   §720.308, F.S.

5.8   Commingling of Association Funds. During the period that the developer controls the board of directors of the homeowners association, all funds of the association must be separately maintained in the association's name, and the operating funds of the association may not be commingled with the reserve funds of the association.[21] The association funds may be used for association purposes, but may not be used by the developer to defend civil or criminal actions, administrative proceeding, or arbitration proceedings that have been filed against the developer or the directors appointed by the developer.[22] After the homeowners assume control of the association's board of directors, reserve and operating funds of the association may be jointly invested; however, such jointly invested funds must be accounted for separately.[23]

5.9   Time for Payment and Delinquency. The timely remittance of assessments and assessment installments from each member is essential to the smooth functioning of the homeowners association and the proper maintenance of the community's property. The association, through its board of directors, has the power to establish and collect the assessments and to additionally establish the time when each assessment or assessment installment is due.[24]

When exercising its authority to set the assessment levels, the board of directors must also establish specific due dates for the assessment or the assessment installments. In addition to a due date, the board should also identify the point in time when the payment becomes delinquent.[25] The payment procedures should be contained in a resolution or in the minutes of the board of directors meeting. They should also be included in the

---

[21]   §720.303 (8) (b), F.S.
[22]   §720.303 (8) (c), F.S.
[23]   §720.303 (8) (a), F.S.
[24]   §720.301 (1) and §720.303 (6), F.S.
[25]   §720.303 (4) (j) 2., F.S.

assessment notices which are provided to each member of the association. The clarity of the board of directors' actions and the responsibility of each member of the association is an essential ingredient to ensure timely payment by responsible members and to ensure effective enforcement against delinquent members.

5.10 Enforcement and Liens. The enforcement rights which the homeowners association has against delinquent members includes the right to lien the delinquent parcel owner.[26] When exercising the lien rights provided to the homeowners association, the board of directors should evidence its claim by filing a formal "claim of lien" with the appropriate recording officer in the county where the property is located. The claim of lien becomes effective on the date of its recording and continues until the assessment and the costs of collection are paid in full. When the declaration of covenants specifically permits, the lien of the homeowners association for delinquent assessments may take priority over the mortgage of a parcel owner.[27]

The claim of lien should state the legal description of the property, the name of the property owner and the amount and date when the assessment or assessment installment became due. The claim of lien should be signed by an officer or agent of the homeowners association. Once it has been recorded, a registered or certified letter should be delivered to the delin-

---

[26] §720.301 (1) and (11) (b), F.S.; *see also Bessemer v. Gersten, supra* at note 14.

[27] *Holly Lake Ass'n v. Federal National Mortgage Ass'n,* 660 So.2d 266 (Fla. 1995) *citing New York Life Insurance & Annuity Corp. v. Hammocks Community Assoc.,* 622 So.2d 1369 (Fla. 3d DCA 1993). The superiority in lien rights relies on specific language in the declaration. *See Ass'n of Poinciana Villages v. Avatar Properties, Inc.,* 724 So.2d 585 (Fla. 5th DCA 1998) and *Federal National Mortgage Ass'n v. McKesson,* 639 So.2d 78 (Fla. 4th DCA 1994).

quent parcel owner with a copy of the lien and a statement of the interest and costs which the lien secures.

In addition to its lien rights, the association has other available sanctions which it may impose against delinquent parcel owners if the governing documents provide for them. The law permits fines and the suspension of a member's rights to use the common areas in the community. When permitted, the documents of the association may also suspend the voting rights of a member for the nonpayment of regular annual assessments that are delinquent for more than ninety (90) days.[28]

When an owner is delinquent in his or her financial obligation to the homeowners association, the remaining association members assume an unfair share of the community's financial responsibilities. As a result, the board of directors should not be reluctant to use the collection sanctions which the community documents allow.

5.11 Annual Financial Report. Each year the board of directors must provide, by mail or personal delivery to all members, a copy of the association's annual financial report or a written notice that a copy of the report is available upon request at no charge to the member.[29] The financial report must consist of financial statements presented in conformity with generally accepted accounting principles based upon the total annual revenue of the association.[30]

The board of directors is required to prepare the appropriate annual financial report within sixty (60) days after the close of the fiscal year of the association,[31] and the board must pro-

---

28 §720.305 (2) and (3), F.S.
29 *Romero v. Shadywood Villas Homeowners Association, Inc.* 657 So.2d 1193 (Fla. 3d DCA 1995).
30 §720.303 (7) (a)., F.S.
31 *Id.*

vide the report or the required notice of its availability to the members of the homeowners association within ten (10) business days of its completion.[32]

An association with total annual revenues between $100,000 and $200,000 is required to prepare compiled financial statements. An association with total annual revenues between $200,000 and $400,000 is required to prepare reviewed financial statements, and an association with total annual revenues of $400,000 or more is required to prepare audited financial statements.[33] Associations that have annual revenues of less than $100,000 are only required to prepare a report of cash receipts and expenditures, and an association of fewer than fifty (50) parcels may prepare a report consisting of only cash receipts and expenditures, regardless of the annual revenues, unless the governing documents of the association require otherwise.[34]

By petition, twenty (20) percent of the association membership may require the board of directors to call a special meeting of the membership to consider a higher level of financial reporting than the minimum level of reporting required by law. Within thirty (30) days of receipt of the petition, the board of directors is required to notice and hold a membership meeting to consider the petition. If the higher level of reporting is approved by a majority of the total voting interests of the association, the board shall make the necessary funds available for the modified financial report, and the report shall be completed and available within ninety (90) days.[35]

The association membership may also provide for a lower level of reporting upon a majority vote of the members present at a properly called membership meeting, but the association

---

[32] §720.303 (5), F.S.

[33] *Id.*

[34] §720.303 (7) (b)., F.S.

[35] §720.303 (7) (c), F.S.

must, at a minimum, provide a report of the cash receipts and expenditures.[36] The report of the cash receipts and expenditures is required to disclose the amounts of all receipts by account and classification, as well as the amounts of expenses by account and classification.[37]

5.12 Annual Financial Filings. In addition to the annual financial report, two additional financial filings are required annually of Florida homeowners associations. Each homeowners association, whether organized for profit or not-for-profit, is required to file an annual corporate report with Florida's Division of Corporations.[38] The annual report is required to maintain the association in an active status and in good standing under Florida corporate law. Each association is also required to file an annual income tax return with the Internal Revenue Service.[39] A corporation organized not-for-profit is neither tax exempt nor exempt from filing an annual tax return.

5.13 Contracts for Products and Services. Any contract for the purchase or lease of materials or equipment that cannot be performed within one (1) year and all contracts for the provision of services to the homeowners association are required to be in writing. Additionally, any contract for materials or equipment or for the provision of services that requires payments by the association that exceed ten (10) percent of the total annual budget of the association, including reserves, must be competitively bid by the board of directors.[40]

The board is not required to accept the lowest bid,[41] and competitive bidding requirements do not limit the association's

---

[36] §720.303 (7) (d), F.S.

[37] §720.303 (7) (b) 3, F.S.

[38] §617.1622, F.S.

[39] The tax returns of the homeowners' association are part of the financial and accounting records of the association. §720.303 (4) (j) 3., F.S.

[40] §720.3055 (1), F.S.

[41] *Id.*

ability to obtain needed products and services in an emergency.[42] An association whose governing documents specifically provide for competitive bidding will govern the bidding process, provided that the document requirements are not less stringent than the requirements of the law.[43]

Contracts with employees of the homeowners association, and contracts for attorney, accountant, architect, community manager, engineering, and landscape architect services are not required to be competitively bid by the association. When a contract with a manager is competitively bid, however, it may be made for a period of up to three (3) years in length.[44] Contracts for materials and services provided to the association under a local government franchise agreement by the franchise holder, renewal of contracts competitively bid that provide the board may cancel on thirty (30) days notice,[45] and sole source contracts[46] are exempt from competitive bidding requirements.

---

[42] §720.3055 (2) (b), F.S.

[43] §720.3055 (2) (a), F.S.

[44] *Id.*

[45] *Id.*

[46] §720.3055 (2) (c), F.S.

6

Rights and Responsibilities of the Parcel Owner

6.1   General. The declaration of covenants and the other governing documents of the community are for the collective benefit of the members of the homeowners association. They establish the tenor for the community, and they define the rights and responsibilities of the individual association members. The laws governing Florida homeowners associations are intended to support the community concept established by the governing documents while protecting the rights of the individual parcel owners.[1]

Each parcel owner is presumed to have knowledge of the community's governing documents, and occupancy of the property in the community by a parcel owner must be consistent with the community concept. Under the law and the declaration of covenants, the owner of a parcel enjoys numerous rights and benefits. They may vary significantly based upon the language of an individual community's documents, but each owner is entitled to rely upon the content of the governing documents and the benefits conferred in them concerning the use of property in the community. These rights and benefits are appurtenances to the ownership of a parcel and run with the land.[2]

6.2   Use of the Common Area. The right to use the easements, common areas and recreational amenities in accordance with the purposes for which they are intended is an appurtenance guaranteed to each parcel owner.[3] The rights of parcel owners and their visitors and guests to use the common areas, however, may not hinder nor unreasonably encroach upon the lawful rights of other parcel owners. By example, speed bumps placed on a private road by a homeowners association have been determined to substantially diminish the rights of individ-

---

[1]   §720.302 (1), F.S.

[2]   *See generally, Hagan v. Sabal Palms, Inc.*, 186 So.2d 302 (Fla. 2d DCA 1966); *Black's Law Dictionary*, 5th Ed. Rev.

[3]   §720.301 (2) and §720.304 (1), F.S.; *see also S & T Anchorage, Inc. v. Lewis*, 575 So.2d 696 (Fla. 3d DCA 1991).

ual owners to use the road and, therefore, constitute an improper or unreasonable restriction on the use of the common area.[4] Similarly, a dock constructed on association-owned property for the benefit of a single parcel owner was also deemed to violate the rights of the other owners entitled to the use and benefit of the common property.[5]

The right of a parcel owner to use the common areas includes the right to peaceably assemble in the common facilities and the right to invite public officers or candidates for public office to appear and speak on the common facilities. Any parcel owner prevented from exercising the rights guaranteed by the law for use of the common areas or recreational facilities may petition the Department of Business and Professional Regulation for mandatory mediation to protect those rights[6] and may bring a civil action to enforce the rights guaranteed parcel owners if the mediation is unsuccessful.[7]

The rights of a parcel owner to use common areas and facilities may be denied for a reasonable period of time if the governing documents of the homeowners association authorize the suspension of these rights for violations of the community's covenants and restrictions.[8] Rights of an owner to use the common facilities may also be suspended for delinquent assessments when the governing documents permit.[9] The suspension of use rights to the common areas may not, however, impair the right of a parcel owner or the tenant of a parcel to have vehicular and pedestrian ingress and egress to and from the parcel, including the right to park an authorized motor vehicle.[10]

---

[4]   *Monell v. Golfview Road Ass'n*, 359 So.2d 2 (Fla. 4th DCA 1978).
[5]   *Johnson v. Tlush*, 468 So.2d 1023 (Fla. 4th DCA 1985).
[6]   §720.305 (2) (a), F.S.
[7]   §720.305 (1), F.S.; *see also Lewis v. S & T Anchorage, Inc.*, 616 So.2d 478 (Fla. 3d DCA 1993).
[8]   §720.305 (2), F.S.
[9]   §720.305 (2) (b), F.S.
[10] §720.305 (2) (c), F.S.

6.3   Guests and Tenants of a Parcel Owner. The guests and tenants of a member of the association are covered by the provisions of the governing documents for the community and the law governing homeowners associations in Florida.[11] As such, they enjoy the rights to use and occupy the common areas and property in the community in the manner authorized by the documents.[12]

Guests and tenants are also required to comply with the covenants, restrictions and rules of the association governing the use of the properties in the community.[13] The failure of a guest or tenant to comply with the community's governing documents subjects the individual parcel owner to possible proceedings before the Department of Business and Professional Regulation, court action and other sanctions for any violation which they commit.[14] (See 7.4 and 7.5.)

6.4   Membership and Voting Rights in the Association. Every parcel owner or the owner's agent is entitled to membership in the homeowners association designated by the declaration of covenants as the managing entity for the community.[15] Each association member is distributed a voting interest by the governing documents as an appurtenance to membership in the homeowners association,[16] and the voting rights of a member may not be suspended by the association unless specifically authorized by the governing documents for the nonpayment of regular annual assessments.[17] (See 5.9.) Unless the governing

---

11   §720.305 (1), F.S.
12   §720.305 (2) (c), F.S.
13   §720.305 (1), F.S.
14   §720.305 (1) (d) and (2), F.S.
15   §720.301 (9) and (10), F.S.
16   §720.301 (13), F.S.; *see also Villages at Mango Key v. Hunter Development, Inc.,* 763 So.2d 476 (Fla. 5th DCA 2000).
17   §720.305 (2) (d), F.S.

documents provide otherwise, membership in the association extends to each owner of a parcel having multiple owners.

Members of the homeowners association have all of the voting rights granted them by the governing documents for the community.[18] Additionally, as a member of the association, there are certain related rights and privileges guaranteed to each member by statute. Association members are eligible to be nominated to, and serve as a member of, the board of directors of the homeowners association.[19] Members are entitled to receive prior notice of all meetings of the board of directors[20] and the membership.[21] Copies of the association budget and the annual financial report are available to all members at no charge,[22] and all the records of the association are available for inspection by members at reasonable times and places.[23] (See 6.6.)

6.5 Participation in Association Affairs. No member of the homeowners association may act on behalf of the association simply by reason of being a member,[24] but each member has the right to participate in important parts of the association's decision-making processes. All members have the right to attend and participate in all meetings of the membership and to exercise their voting interest, either in person or by proxy, on any and all decisions made at such meetings, including the selection of directors for the association.[25] When the homeowners association fails to fill enough vacancies on the board to constitute a quorum, it is the right of any member to petition the circuit court for the appointment of a receiver to look after the affairs

---

[18] §720.301 (4), F.S.
[19] §720.306 (9), F.S.
[20] §720.303 (2), F.S.
[21] §720.306 (4), F.S.
[22] §720.303 (8) and (9), F.S.
[23] §720.303 (5), F.S.
[24] §720.303 (1), F.S.; *see also* §617.0604 (1), F.S.
[25] §720.306 (2), (6) and (7), F.S.

of the association until a quorum can be attained.[26] (See 3.3.)

Any member of the association is authorized by law to tape-record or videotape any meetings of the association membership, as well as meetings of the board of directors. The right to record such meetings may be subject to reasonable restrictions provided that the restrictions have been adopted in advance by the board of directors.[27] Members also have the right under the law to place items before the board of directors and to speak on those items when they appear on the agenda of the board meeting.[28] (See 3.12.)

The rights and privileges granted by the governing documents are for the benefit of the community and each member of the community. No amendments may be made to the governing documents unless they are first presented to the members of the association for their approval in accordance with the requirements stated in the documents. If no threshold of approval is stated in the documents, an affirmative vote of two-thirds of the voting interests in the association is required. When an amendment affects vested rights of parcel owners, all owners affected by the change and all affected lien holders must join in the execution of the amendments to the documents.[29] (See 7.10.)

6.6   Access to Association Records. All records of a homeowners association are available to the association members. Before a prospective purchaser becomes a parcel owner and member of the homeowners association, the purchaser must be presented a disclosure summary of the community's governing

---

[26] §720.305 (3), F.S.

[27] §720.306 (10), F.S.

[28] §720.303 (2) (b) and (d), F.S.

[29] §720.306(1)(b) and (c), F.S.; *Palma v. Townhouses of Oriole Ass'n, Inc.*, 610 So.2d 112 (Fla. 4th DCA 1992); *see also Norwood-Norland Homeowners v. Dade County.*, 511 So.2d 1009, 1014 (Fla. 3d DCA 1987).

documents.[30] Upon request, the association is required to provide a complete copy of the recorded governing documents to any association member or prospective purchaser who requests them. The association may charge for the actual costs for reproducing and furnishing the documents to those persons entitled to receive them.[31]

The other official records of the homeowners association are also open to inspection and available for photocopying by members of the association or their authorized representatives.[32] If the association has a copy machine available, it must provide the copies upon request during the inspection if the request is limited to no more than twenty-five (25) pages, and the association may charge up to fifty (50) cents per page for the copies.[33]

When the association does not have a copy machine available or if the request is for more than twenty-five (25) pages, the association may have copies made by an outside vender and may charge the member for the actual cost of the copying.[34] The records of the association must be maintained within the state and must be made available to members or their authorized representatives at reasonable times and places within ten (10) business days after receipt of a written request for access.[35]

The homeowners association may adopt reasonable rules governing the time, location, frequency, notice, and manner of records' inspection, but the rules must be in writing. The rules may not impose a requirement that the parcel owner give a reason or demonstrate a proper purpose for the inspection, nor may

[30] §21, Chapter 2004-345, *Laws of Florida.*
[31] §720.303 (5) (c), F.S.
[32] §720.303 (5), F.S.
[33] *Id.*[34]§720.303 (5) (c), F.S.
[35] §720.303(5), F.S. The failure to provide access to records within 10 business days after receipt of a written request from a member creates a rebuttable presumption that the association willfully failed to provide access to the records.

the rules limit the right to inspect the records to less than one (1) eight-hour business day per month. The homeowners association is not authorized to charge a fee for the inspection of records, but it may impose fees to cover the costs of providing members copies of the official records.[36] If the association denies access to its official records,[37] the member who is denied access is entitled to damages from the association for its willful failure to provide the records.[38]

Some records of the homeowners association are not accessible to members or parcel owners. These records include information obtained by the association in connection with the approval of a sale or other transfer of a parcel, personnel records of association employees, medical records of community residents, and records protected by the attorney-client privilege prepared by the association attorney for pending or imminent litigation.[39]

6.7 Financial Obligations. Every parcel owner, regardless of how title to the property has been acquired, including purchase at a judicial sale, is liable for all assessments or amenity fees which come due while he or she is the owner.[40] Assessments for the community's operations are levied pursuant to the annual budget or special assessment, and they are allocated among the individual members of the homeowners association in the manner described by the community's governing documents. The liability of the owner of a parcel for assessments is limited to the amounts properly assessed against the parcel by the homeowners association.[41]

---

[36] §720.303 (5) (c), F.S.

[37] §720.303 (5) (a), F.S.

[38] §720.303 (5) (b), F.S

[39] §720.303 (5) (c), F.S.

[40] §720.301 (11) (b) 2., F.S.; *see also* §720.312, F.S.

[41] §720.308, F.S.

A current account of the status of each member's financial obligation to the homeowners association must be maintained as a part of the association's official records,[42] and it is available for inspection upon request.[43] Once assessed, the association has a lien on each parcel for any unpaid assessments and for attorney's fees and costs incurred by the association incident to the collection of the assessment or the enforcement of the lien.[44] Failure to pay an assessment may also result in fines or suspension of the right to vote or the right to use the recreational amenities and common areas of the community when the governing documents permit.[45] (See 5.9.)

6.8 Sale and Transfer of the Parcel. The covenants of a homeowners association may not unreasonably restrict the right of a parcel owner to sell or transfer the owner's property.[46] Covenants that attempt to unduly restrict a sale of property are considered to be an "improper restraint on alienation," and they have been deemed void by Florida courts.[47] A parcel owner may not, however, use the right to sell or transfer a portion of the parcel to violate the original intent of the declaration of covenants, and efforts to do so have been rejected by the courts.[48]

Prior to the sale of an individual parcel, prospective purchasers must be provided a disclosure summary of the rights and obligations incident to ownership of a parcel in the community. Any contract for the sale of a lot or parcel must refer to or incorporate the required disclosure summary. The summary

---

[42] §720.303 (4) (j) 2., F.S.

[43] §720.303 (5), F.S.

[44] §720.301 (1), F.S.

[45] §720.305 (2) (b), F.S.

[46] *Brower v. Hubbard*, 643 So.2d 28 (Fla. 4th DCA 1994).

[47] *Camino Gardens Ass'n, Inc. v. McKim*, 612 So.2d 636 (Fla. 4th DCA 1993); *see also Davis v. Geyer*, 9 So.2d 727 (Fla. 1942).

[48] *Royal Oak Landing v. Pelletier*, 620 So.2d 786 (Fla. 4th DCA 1993).

must state that membership in the homeowners association is mandatory and that recorded covenants govern the use and occupancy of property. The disclosure must reveal the obligation to pay assessments which, if unpaid, may result in a lien against the parcel and any fee or rental amounts required for use of common facilities. The summary must also disclose whether or not the recorded covenants may be amended without the approval of the association membership.[49]

Each prospective parcel owner in a new development is entitled to receive the disclosure summary from the developer,[50] and the law provides special remedies for a purchaser who has been the victim of false and misleading information published by the developer.[51] In any contract for the resale of a residential parcel, the disclosure summary must be provided by the seller.[52]

Purchasers of parcels governed by a homeowners association are bound by constructive notice of the restrictive covenants that are imposed upon their property.[53] The restrictions in the recorded covenants and the disclosure summary are clothed with a strong presumption of validity arising from the fact that each parcel owner purchases the parcel knowing of and accepting the restrictions imposed.[54]

6.9 Recreational and Common Facilities Leases. The law imposes certain restrictions and grants to the members certain

---

[49] §21, Chapter 2004-345, *Laws of Florida*.

[50] The developer is the person or entity that creates the community served by the association or succeeds to the rights and liabilities of the person or entity creating the community. §617.301(5), F.S.

[51] §§21and 24, Chapter 2004-345, *Laws of Florida*.

[52] §21, Chapter 2004-345, *Laws of Florida*.

[53] *Daniel v. May*, 143 So.2d 536 (Fla. 2d DCA 1962).

[54] *Eastpointe Prop. Owners' Ass'n v. Cohen*, 504 So.2d 518 (Fla. 4th DCA 1987), *citing Hidden Harbour Estates v. Basso*, 393 So.2d 637 (Fla. 4th DCA 1981).

rights concerning any lease for recreational or other commonly used facilities entered into after June 15, 1995. When the lease has been entered into by the members or the homeowners association before control of the association is turned over to the members other than the developer, the lease may not contain a rent escalation clause based upon a nationally recognized commodity or consumer index. If such a clause is included in a lease entered into after June 15, 1995, the clause is unenforceable.[55] The lease must also extend certain rights to the members of the homeowners association to acquire the leased property through the association.

When the owner of the leased facilities wishes to sell the property, it may not be offered for sale unless the association is first granted a ninety (90) day option to purchase the property. Within the option period, a purchase contract must be executed by the parties or the owner of the facility may sell the property to another party.[56]

If the owner of the facilities receives an unsolicited offer to purchase the property that the owner intends to consider or make a counteroffer, the owner is obligated to notify the homeowners association that the offer has been received. The notice must be mailed to the president of the association,[57] and it must disclose the purchase price and the material terms and conditions of the proposed sale. The facility owner is not obligated to sell the property to the association, but the owner is obligated to consider any purchase offer that is made by the homeowners association.[58]

---

[55]   §720.31 (5), F.S.
[56]   *Id.*
[57]§720.31 (3), F.S.
[58]   §720.31 (2), F.S.

6.10 Display of Flags. Florida law makes specific provision for the display of the United States flag and the official flag of the State of Florida by property owners in the community, and the declaration of covenants, articles of incorporation and bylaws of the homeowners association may not preclude such a display. On Memorial Day, Flag Day, Independence Day, Veterans Day and Armed Forces Day, members may also display official flags of the United States Army, Navy, Air Force, Marine Corps, or Coast Guard.[59]

Authorized flags must be displayed in a respectful manner, and the association may establish reasonable standards governing the size, placement and safety of the display, consistent with Title 36 U.S.C., Chapter 10 and any applicable local ordinances.[60] Official flags of the designated branches of the United States military may not be larger than four (4) feet by six (6) feet and must be portable and removable.[61]

6.11 Display of Signs. It is not uncommon to find provisions in the governing documents of the homeowners association that restrict the placement of signs on parcels in the community. These covenant provisions are enforceable when they are clear and unambiguous,[62] and when they are consistent with the contemplated purpose of the sign restrictions.[63] Notwithstanding restrictions in the documents, however, a parcel owner is permitted by law to display a sign of reasonable size that has been provided by a contractor for security services within ten (10) feet of any entrance to the home located on the parcel.[64]

---

[59] §720.304 (2), F.S.

[60] §720.3075 (3), F.S.

[61] §720.304 (2), F.S.

[62] *Shields v. Andros Isles Property Owners Ass'n, Inc.*, 872 So.2d 1003 (Fla. 4th DCA 2004).

[63] *Wilson v. Rex Quality Corporation*, 839 So.2d 928 (Fla. 2th DCA 2003).

[64] §720.304 (6), F.S.

6.12 Access Ramp Construction. Notwithstanding contrary provisions in the governing documents of the community, it is the right of any parcel owner to construct an access ramp for ingress and egress to the home when a resident or occupant has a disability or medical necessity requiring the modified access.[65] Prior to construction of the access ramp, the parcel owner is required to submit plans for the proposed ramp to the board of directors,[66] together with a physician's affidavit verifying the disability or medical condition.[67]

The board of directors may not reject the application, but may make reasonable requests to the parcel owner to modify the design in order to achieve architectural consistency with surrounding structures. The parcel owner is expected to provide a design for the access ramp that is as unobtrusive as possible and reasonably sized to fit the intended use.[68]

6.13 SLAPP Protection and Public Participation. The law provides owners in the community with special protections to exercise their rights of free speech before institutions of government on matters related to the homeowners association and from "strategic lawsuits against public participation," known as SLAPP suits, when they engage in the participation.[69] SLAPP suits by any individual or business organization against a parcel owner are prohibited,[70] and a homeowners association is specifically prohibited from using association funds to prosecute a SLAPP suit against a parcel owner.[71]

When a SLAPP suit is filed against a parcel owner, the owner may petition the court for an order dismissing the action.[72] The court is required to set a hearing on the dismissal

---

[65] §720.304 (5) (a), F.S.
[66] *Id.*[67]§720.304 (5) (b), F.S.
[68] §720.304 (5) (a), F.S.
[69] §720.304 (4), F.S.
[70] §720.304 (4) (a), F.S.
[71] §720.304 (4) (c), F.S.
[72] §720.304 (4) (b), F.S.

request at the earliest possible time, and if the parcel owner is successful, the judge may award treble damages to a prevailing owner, together with attorney's fees and costs against the person or business entity bringing the action in violation of the SLAPP suit prohibition.[73]

6.14 Electronic Transmission of Notices. With the consent of the homeowner and if permitted by the association bylaws, notices for meetings of the board of directors, for committee meetings, and for regular and special meetings of the membership may be transmitted electronically.[74] The exception to this notice option is a meeting of the membership where the recall of a board member or members will be considered, and the electronic method of giving notice may not be used for these meetings.[75]

Electronic transmission includes both computer e-mail and facsimile transmission,[76] and notice is properly given when transmitted to the number, e-mail address or electronic network provided to the association by the homeowner.[77] An affidavit of the secretary or other authorized agent of the association that the notice has been given by electronic transmission is, in the absence of fraud, prima facia evidence of the facts stated in the notice.[78]

---

[73] *Id.*
[74] §720.303 (2), F.S.
[75] §720.303 (10) (c), F.S.
[76] 617.01401 (6), F.S.
[77] 617.0141 (3), F.S.
[78] §617.0141 (8), F.S.

7

Covenants and Use of Association Property

7.1 Covenants. Covenants governing the use of property in a community may range from the obligation to pay a portion of the common expenses to restrictions on what may be placed upon and who may occupy an individual parcel.[1] The covenants may impose limitations on the use of the property by requiring the performance of certain duties or guaranteeing certain rights to the owners of the property. Each parcel owner subject to the covenants of a homeowners association is presumed to have knowledge of the restrictions and the responsibilities that the covenants impose.[2] Additionally, each parcel owner has the right to enforce the covenants of the homeowners association against any other member, the association or any director or officer of the association who willfully and knowingly fails to comply with the governing documents.[3]

There are essentially two categories of covenants or restrictions. The first category consists of those restrictions found in the recorded instrument subjecting the community to the jurisdiction of the homeowners association known as the "declaration of covenants."[4] The second category consists of those restrictions that are promulgated by the board of directors pursuant to authority granted by the governing documents. The first category of restrictions is clothed with a strong presumption of validity because each parcel owner purchases his or her property knowing and accepting the restrictions to be imposed.[5]

---

[1] *Wood v. McElvey*, 296 So.2d 102 (Fla. 2d DCA 1974); *Voight v. Harbour Heights Improvement Ass'n*, 218 So.2d 803 (Fla. 4th DCA 1969); and *Rocek v. Markowitz*, 492 So.2d 460 (Fla. 5th DCA 1986).

[2] *Hagan v. Sabal Palms, Inc.*, 186 So.2d 302, 312-13 (Fla. 2d DCA 1966); *Eastpointe Prop. Owners Ass'n v. Cohen*, 504 So.2d 518 (Fla. 4th DCA 1987).

[3] §720.305 (1), F.S.; *see also Loch Haven Homeowners' Ass'n v. Nelle*, 389 So.2d 697 (Fla. 2d DCA 1980).

[4] §720.301 (4), F.S.

[5] *Shields v. Andros Isles Property Owners Ass'n, Inc.*, 872 So.2d 1003 (Fla. 4th DCA 2004).

Restrictions in the second category must meet a test of reasonableness which tempers the discretion of the board of directors.[6]

7.2 Covenants for Operation and Maintenance. Portions of the governing documents establish the responsibility for the operation and management of the community with the homeowners association[7] and provide for the maintenance and management of the common properties and easements in the community.[8] When the documents permit, the association may also enter and repair the property of an individual parcel owner when the owner fails to do so.[9] These covenants providing for the operation, maintenance or management of the association or the property in the community must be fair and reasonable.[10]

The law governing homeowners associations imposes the same "fair and reasonable" standard on all contracts with a term in excess of ten (10) years and made by the association for operation, maintenance or management before control of the association is turned over to the members other than the developer.[11]

The law also makes certain other restrictive covenants concerning the operation and maintenance of the community unenforceable. Association covenants may not prohibit display of the United States flag, the flag of the State of Florida or flags of the United States Armed Services on designated holidays. The association may, however, place reasonable restrictions may govern the size and placement of the flag.[12] (See 6.10.)

Any restrictive covenant appearing in a community's gov-

---

6   *Eastpointe Prop. Owners' Ass'n v. Cohen, supra* note 2 at page 520.

7   §720.301 (9), F.S.

8   §720.301 (1) and (4), F.S.; *see also Secret Oaks Owner's Ass'n v. D.E.P.,* 704 So.2d 702 (Fla. 5th DCA 1998).

9   *Demaio v. Coco Wood Lakes Ass'n, Inc.,* 637 So.2d 369 (Fla. 4th DCA 1994).

10   §720.309, F.S.

11   *Id.*

12   §720.304 (2), F.S.; *see also* §720.3075 (3), F.S.

erning documents that attempts to prohibit the installation of solar collectors, clotheslines or other energy devices based on renewable energy resources is contrary to public policy.[13] A homeowners association may not enforce such restrictions, and in any litigation to protect the right to install energy-saving devices, the prevailing party is entitled to recover court costs and reasonable attorney's fees.[14] Additionally, governing documents for communities created after October 1, 2001, may not prohibit any parcel owner from implementing Xeriscape or "Florida friendly landscape."[15] "Florida friendly landscape" means quality landscapes that conserve water and protect the environment, are adaptable to local conditions and which are drought tolerant.[16] Parcel owners may also install access ramps for disabled occupants of the property when necessary for ingress and egress.[17] (See 6.11.)

7.3 Compliance with the Covenants and Restrictions.

The provisions of the declaration of covenants are enforceable as equitable servitudes, and they are covenants and restrictions with which the association, each officer and director of the association, and each parcel owner and their visitors and guests must comply.[18] The declaration of covenants is also binding upon the developer and upon each subsequent parcel owner in the community.[19]

The uniqueness of community living and the resultant necessity for a greater degree of control over the rights of the

---

[13] §163.04 (2), F.S.

[14] §163.04 (3), F.S.

[15] §720.3075 (4), F.S.

[16] §373.185 (1)(b), F.S.

[17] §720.304 (5) (a), F.S.

[18] §720.305 (1), F.S.

[19] *Blue Reef Holding Corp., Inc. v. Coyne*, 645 So.2d 1053, 1055 (Fla. 4th DCA 1994).

individual parcel owners than might be tolerated given more traditional forms of property ownership is one of the basic principles of the homeowners association concept.[20] As a matter of equity, however, the courts have refused to sustain restrictions under circumstances which render their enforcement inequitable.[21]

Although the declaration of covenants is strictly construed in favor of a parcel owner's free use of his or her property,[22] when covenants have been clearly stated, and their enforcement is not unreasonable or arbitrary, the restrictions have been determined to be valid.[23] When the provisions of deed restrictions are discretionary, an association is not permitted to establish standards that are more restrictive than those permitted by local building codes.[24] Neither is the association permitted to stretch the meaning of the terms used in the community's covenants when the language is otherwise clear and unambiguous.[25]

All valid provisions of the declaration of covenants relating to a parcel that has been sold for taxes or special assessments survive the sale. The covenants are enforceable after the

---

[20] *Belle Terre Ass'n Inc. v. Brosch*, 216 So.2d 462 (Fla. 2d DCA 1968); *see also Monahan v. Homeowner's of La Cita, Inc.*, 622 So.2d 551 (Fla. 5th DCA 1993) restricting the storage of a motor home on a parcel owner's property.

[21] *Flamingo Ranch Estates v. Sunshine Ranches Homeowners' Ass'n*, 303 So.2d 665 (Fla. 4th DCA 1974).

[22] *Moore v. Stevens*, 106 So.2d 901 (Fla. 1925); *see also Moss v. Inverness Highlands Civic Ass'n*, 521 So.2d 359 (Fla. 5th DCA 1988); *Monahan v. Homeowner's of La Cita, Inc., supra* note 15.

[23] *Engvalson v. Webster*, 74 So.2d 113 (Fla. 1954); *see also Lathan v. Hanover Woods Homeowners Ass'n*, 547 So.2d 319 (Fla. 5th DCA 1989) where authority was not clearly stated and *Klak v. Eaglesi Reserve Homeowners Assín, Inc.*, 862 So.2d 947 (Fla. 2d DCA 2004) where court did not apply clear meaning of covenant.

[24] *Voight v. Harbour Heights Improvement Ass'n, supra* note 1.

[25] *Heck v. Parkview Place Homeowners Association, Inc.*, 642 So.2d 1201 (Fla. 4th DCA 1994).

issuance of a tax deed or upon foreclosure of an assessment to the same extent that they would be enforceable by or against a voluntary purchaser of the parcel.[26] A homeowners association may also preserve the community's covenants and restrictions under Florida's Marketable Record Title Act[27] by filing notice of the extension of the covenants with the Clerk of the Circuit Court. The notice and extension must be approved by a two-thirds vote of the board of directors at a meeting where a quorum is present and notice has been provided to each member of the association at least 7 days prior to the meeting.[28] The declaration of covenants may also be revived after expiring under the procedures established by Chapter 720 of the Florida Statutes.[29] (See 7.11.)

7.4 Mediation and Enforcement of the Documents. The board of directors of the homeowners association has the statutory authority to enforce the governing documents and the rules of the association when a violation occurs.[30] Each individual member of the association also has the authority to enforce the documents and the association rules.[31]

Disputes between a parcel owner and the association regarding (1) the use of or changes to the owner's parcel or the common areas, (2) covenant disputes, (3) disputes regarding

---

[26] §720.312, F.S.; *see Gainer v. Fiddlesticks County Club, Inc.*, 710 So.2d 76 (Fla. 2d DCA 1998).

[27] Chapter 712, F.S.

[28] §712.05, F.S.; *see also Cudjoe Gardens Property Owners Assoc., Inc. v. Payne*, 770 So.2d 190 (Fla. 3d DCA 2001).

[29] §§7 and 8, Chapter 2004-345, *Laws of Florida*.

[30] Prior to the 1995 law authorizing an association to enforce community documents, the Supreme Court of Florida declined to permit an association standing to enforce covenants when it was not the direct successor to the developer's interests or expressly assigned the right to enforce the documents. *See Palm Point Property Owners' Association of Charlotte County, Inc. v. Pisarski*, 626 So.2d 195 (Fla. 1993).

[31] §720.305 (1), F.S.

meetings of the board and committees of the board, (4) meetings of the membership not involving elections, and (5) access to the official records of the association must be submitted to the Department of Business and Professional Regulation for mandatory mediation before the dispute is filed in court.[32] Election disputes and disputes over the recall of a member or members of the board of directors are not eligible for mediation, and these matters must be submitted to the Department for mandatory binding arbitration.[33] Any petition for mediation or arbitration filed with the Department tolls any statute of limitations that might be applicable to the dispute.[34]

Mediation proceedings are conducted in accordance with the Florida Rules of Civil Procedure and the proceedings are privileged and confidential. Persons who are not parties to the dispute may not attend the mediation without the consent of the parties, and when mediation is attended by a quorum of the board of directors, it is not considered a board meeting for purposes of notice and membership participation under the law.[35]

The party filing a mediation petition is required to pay a $200.00 filing fee, and unless the parties otherwise agree, the costs of the mediation proceedings shall be charged equally to the parties at the conclusion of the proceedings. The cost shall include the initial filing fee and the fees charged by the mediator.[36]

If the mediation proceedings are not successful in resolving all the issues between the parties, the parties may file the unresolved dispute in either county or circuit court[37] or elect to enter into binding or non-binding arbitration to be conducted by the Department. If all the parties to the dispute do not agree to the arbitration following unsuccessful mediation, or if the dis-

---

[32] §720.311 (2) (a), F.S.

[33] §720.306 (9), F.S. and §720.303 (10), F.S.

[34] §720.311 (1), F.S.

[35] §720.311 (2) (a), F.S.

[36] *Id.*

[37] §34.01 (1) (d), F.S.

pute is not eligible for mediation or arbitration, the association or the member may seek relief in a court action, at law or in equity,[38] and the prevailing party in such action is entitled to recovery of reasonable attorney's fees and costs of the proceeding.[39] At any time after the filing of a complaint in court, the judge may also order the parties to the dispute to enter into further mediation or arbitration proceedings.[40]

7.5 Enforcement Sanctions and Penalties. When the governing documents of the community permit, the board of directors may suspend, for a reasonable period of time, the rights of a member or a member's tenants or guests to use the common areas or recreational facilities for violation of the documents or rules of the association. When permitted by the governing documents, the association may also impose reasonable fines, not to exceed $100 per violation, against any member, tenant or guest violating the rules or the governing documents. An authorized fine may be levied on the basis of each day of a continuing violation, except that the total fine cannot exceed $1,000 in the aggregate unless otherwise provided in the governing documents, and the fine cannot become a lien against the parcel.[41]

Prior to imposing either a fine or suspension, a hearing must be held to afford the alleged violator an opportunity to be heard on the issue. At least fourteen (14) days notice of the hearing must be given, and the hearing must be held before a committee of at least three members of the homeowners associ-

---

[38] §720.311 (2) (b), F.S.

[39] *Id.; Zerquera v. Centennial Homeownersi Assín, Inc.,* 752 So.2d 694 (Fla. 3d DCA 2000). *See also Loch Ness Homeowners Ass'n v. Pelaez,* 730 So.2d 380 (Fla. 3d DCA 1999) *citing Pelican Bay Homeowners Ass'n, Inc. v. Sedita,* 724 So.2d 684 (Fla. 5th DCA 1999).

[40] §720.311, F.S.

[41] §720.305 (2), F.S.

ation appointed by the board of directors who are not officers, directors or employees of the association or the spouse, parent, child, brother or sister of an officer, director or employee of the association. A majority of the committee must affirmatively vote to impose the fine or suspension,[42] and no suspension of the common-area-use rights may impair the right of an owner or tenant to have vehicular or pedestrian ingress and egress to and from the community.[43]

7.6   Notice of Violation and Uniform, Timely Enforcement.
The recorded declaration of covenants and the other documents governing the community are basically an elaborate set of contract terms.[44] Each owner is protected by the contract and may insist on the enforcement of the terms of the documents which protect the individual owner's rights in a uniform and timely manner. Under some circumstances, the homeowners association may be liable for its failure to enforce covenants governing the community or for its decision to waive covenants or restrictions.[45]

The doctrines of estoppel and laches are applicable against a person who sits by and watches while his or her rights or property are encroached upon.[46] Equitable estoppel is a basic concept of fairness that results in a forfeiture of the enforce-

---

[42]   §720.305 (2) (a), F.S.

[43]   §720.305 (2) (c), F.S.

[44]   *Silver Blue Lakes Apartments v. Silver Blue Lake Homeowners' Ass'n*, 245 So.2d 609 (Fla. 1971) ("The theory adopted in this state is that the contract which embodies the restriction may be enforced against both the promisor and those taking from him with notice, thereby including amongst those who may enforce the obligation not only the promise, but those who take from him and those in the neighborhood who may be considered as beneficiaries of the contract.").

[45]   *Barefield v. Lafayette Oaks Homes Ass'n*, 422 So.2d 969 (Fla. 1st DCA 1982). *See also Estates of Fort Lauderdale Property Owners' Ass'n v. Kalet*, 492 So.2d 1340 (Fla. 4th DCA 1986) providing for enforcement after transition from developer control.

[46]   *Monell v. Golfview Road Ass'n*, 359 So.2d 2 (Fla. 4th DCA 1978).

ment rights when they are not used in a timely fashion. Once knowledge of a violation is obtained, enforcement procedures must be implemented without unreasonable delay. If this does not occur in a timely manner, the rights of a parcel owner or the homeowners association to enforce the covenants may be lost.

There is no specific definition for "timely enforcement," and the facts of each case will determine whether the response by the enforcing authority was timely and reasonable under the circumstances. To avoid the issue of untimely enforcement, procedures for prompt response to violations of the community's documents should be adopted and followed by the board of directors.[47]

Uniform treatment of community residents is also essential to successful enforcement of the governing documents. The enforcement procedures of the homeowners association must be uniform, reasonable and consistent, or they can be attacked as arbitrary and capricious, and enforcement will be unsuccessful. When a parcel owner challenges the enforcement of covenants, the owner has the burden to prove the defenses that preclude enforcement, such as a claim that the enforcing authority has acted in an unreasonable or arbitrary manner.[48]

7.7 Architectural Standards. A purchaser's notice of building restrictions may be derived from the deed restrictions themselves or by the visible presence of a unified scheme of development.[49] Florida law has consistently upheld the power of

---

[47] *Loch Ness Homeowners Ass'n, Inc. v. Pelaez, supra* note 27.

[48] *Killearn Acres Homeowners v. Keever*, 595 So.2d 1019 (Fla. 1st DCA 1992).

[49] *Young v. Tortoise Island Homeowners' Ass'n*, 511 So.2d 381 (Fla. 5th DCA 1987).

homeowners associations to enforce building restrictions,[50] even when sales agents misrepresent the extent of or enforcement of the restrictions.[51]

The homeowners association or another parcel owner is fully empowered to seek the removal of structures erected in violation of clearly expressed restrictions.[52] Courts have ordered the removal of such structures and improvements not authorized by the community's covenants, including unauthorized carports,[53] porches,[54] decks,[55] satellite dishes,[56] ham radio antennas,[57] radio tower/antennas,[58] docks,[59] exterior awnings,[60]

---

[50] *Id. See also Coral Gables Investment v. Graham Companies,* 528 So.2d 989 (Fla. 3d DCA 1988); *Engvalson et ux v. Webster,* 74 So.2d 113 (Fla. 1954).

[51] *Esplanade Patio Homes Homeowners' Assoc. v. Rolle,* 613 So.2d 531 (Fla. 3d DCA 1993).

[52] "Where contracts are clear and unambiguous, they should be construed as written, and the court can give it no other meaning." *Heck v. Parkview Place Homeowners Association, Inc., supra* note 20.

[53] *Pelican Island Property Owners' Ass'n v. Murphy,* 554 So.2d 1179 (Fla. 2d DCA 1989).

[54] *Europco Mgt. Co. of America v. Smith,* 572 So.2d 963 (Fla. 1st DCA 1990).

[55] *Miami Lakes Civic Assín, Inc. v. Encinosa,* 699 So.2d 271 (Fla. 3d DCA 1997).

[56] *Killearn Acres Homeowners Association, Inc. v. Keever, supra* note 34; see also *Esplanade Patio Homes v. Rolle, supra* note 37 and *Latera v. The Isle at Mission Bay Homeowners Ass'n,* 655 So.2d 144, (Fla. 4th DCA 1995).

[57] *Emerald Estates Community Assoc., Inc. v. Gorodetzer,* 819 So.2d 190 (Fla. 4th DCA 2002)

[58] *Brower v. Hubbard,* 643 So.2d 28 (Fla. 4th DCA 1994).

[59] *Johnson v. Tlush,* 468 So.2d 1023 (Fla. 4th DCA 1985).

[60] *Eastpointe Property Owners' Ass'n Inc. v. Cohen, supra* note 2.

sheds,[61] improper fencing,[62] concrete walls,[63] an exterior wall plaque,[64] and a portion of a dwelling encroaching on a setback line between parcels.[65] The association's role in enforcing the restrictions also applies to holding the developer accountable for any construction defects in the common areas.[66] (See 1.13.)

A community's covenants notwithstanding, the Telecommunications Act of 1996 assures residential parcel owners access to certain television service provided by "direct broadcast satellite." In response to this mandate from Congress, the Federal Communications Commission has adopted rules that prohibit the enforcement of covenants that restrict, delay or unreasonably increase the cost of installation of a direct broadcast satellite dish which is less than one (1) meter in diameter. The FCC rule makes such covenants affecting property within the exclusive use and ownership of a parcel owner unenforceable.[67]

Restrictions designed to create and maintain a uniform scheme of community development through the discretionary review of the homeowners association are also presumed valid provided such review is properly conducted.[68] The review of

---

61 *McMillan v. The Oaks of Spring Hill Homeowners' Ass'n,* 754 So.2d 160 (Fla. 5th DCA 2000).

62 *James v. Smith,* 537 So.2d 1074 (Fla. 5th DCA 1989).

63 *Velickovich v. Ricci,* 391 So.2d 258 (Fla. 4th DCA 1980).

64 *Lakeridge Greens Homeowners Assoc., Inc. v. Silberman,* 765 So.2d 95 (Fla. 4th DCA 2000).

65 *Daniel v. May,* 143 So.2d 536 (Fla. 3d DCA 1962).

66 *Strathmore Gate-East at Lake St. George Homeowners' v. Levitt Homes,* 537 So.2d 657 (Fla. 2d DCA 1989). *See also* §§558.001-005, F.S.

67 *§25.104, Rules of the Federal Communications Commission* implementing §207 of the Federal Telecommunications Act of 1996.

68 *Cohen v. Boca Woods Country Club Property Owners Ass'n, Inc.,* 632 So.2d 1142 (Fla. 4th DCA 1994); *Young v. Tortoise Island Homeowners' Ass'n, supra* note 35; *Coral Gables Investment v. Graham Companies, supra* note 36; *Voight v. Harbour Heights Improvement Ass'n, supra* note 1; *Engvalson et ux. v Webster, supra* note 36.

proposed structures and improvements for conformity with uniform standards and construction criteria is deemed to be proper when it is exercised in a reasonable manner.[69] However, restrictions based purely on aesthetic concepts,[70] not supported by competent and substantial evidence or establishing arbitrary standards[71] are not valid. Florida law also permits a parcel owner to install access ramps for disabled occupants of the parcel and limits the board's review and approval to consistency with the surrounding structures.[72]

It is permissible for the uniform scheme to be enforced by the board of directors of the homeowners association or by a properly established architectural review committee of the association.[73] Any body, such as an architectural review committee, vested with the power to approve or disapprove architectural decisions with respect to a specific parcel of residential property owned by a member of the community must comply with all the notice and meeting procedures required of the board of directors of the homeowners association.[74] Although the meetings of the board or committee must be open to the members of the association, due process does not require that the affected parcel owner be afforded an opportunity to make a presentation before the decision-making body.[75]

---

[69]   *Id.   See also Emerald Estates Community Assoc., Inc. v. Gorodetzer, supra note 45.*

[70]   *Young v. Tortoise Island Homeowners' Ass'n, supra* note 35; *Coral Gables Investment v. Graham Companies, supra* note 36; *Voight v. Harbour Heights Improvement Ass'n, supra* note 1.

[71]   *Voight v. Harbour Heights Improvement Ass'n, supra* note 1; *Kies v. Hollub,* 450 So.2d 251 (Fla. 3d DCA 1984).

[72]   §720.304 (5) (a), F.S.

[73]   *Holiday Pines Prop. Owners v. Wetherington,* 596 So.2d 84 (Fla. 4th DCA 1992).

[74]   §720.303 (2), F.S.

[75]   *Europco Mgt. Co. of America v. Smith, supra* note 40.

If the local county and municipal building code requires the architectural review committee of the association to approve building design plans as a prerequisite to receiving a building permit, the committee is required to comply with Florida's Government in the Sunshine Law and Public Records Law.[76] As such, meetings of the committee must be noticed and open to the public at large and not merely to members of the association.[77] Records made or received in conjunction with the committee's deliberations are open and available for inspection by the public.[78]

7.8 Age and Occupancy Limitations. Restrictions limiting the use of parcels within a planned development for residential purposes are enforceable and commonplace. Covenants prohibiting the further subdivision of a residential parcel[79] and restricting a parcel to only one residence have also been sustained.[80] A covenant restricting a parcel "for residence only," however, does not prohibit short-term rentals[81] or the erection of a multi-family residential facility.[82] It has been held that a "residential purposes" restriction does not prohibit parcel owners from renting rooms as an adult congregate living facility when the owner of the parcel is also in occupancy.[83] Under a similar covenant where the owner was not in occupancy, however, use of the parcel for an adult congregate living facility was deemed

---

[76] *Advisory Opinion of the Florida Attorney General*, AGO 99-53.

[77] §286.011, F.S.

[78] §119.011 (1), F.S.

[79] *Belle Terre Ass'n v. Brosch*, 216 So.2d 463 (Fla. 2d DCA 1969).

[80] *Mayes v. Hale*, 82 Fla. 35, 89 So. 364 (Fla. 1921). *See also Dornbach v. Holley*, 854 So.2d 211(Fla. 2d DCA 2002) permitting a community residential home and overriding the community covenants.

[81] *Berry v. Teves*, 752 So.2d 112 (Fla. 2d DCA 2000).

[82] *Don Cesar Property Owners Corp. v. Gallagher*, 452 So.2d 1047 (Fla. 2d DCA 1984).

[83] *Moss v. Inverness Highlands South and West Civic Ass'n, Inc.*, 521 So.2d 359 (Fla. 5th DCA 1988).

to be a commercial venture, and its continuation as a congregate facility was enjoined.[84]

Some residential communities are intended for senior adult occupancy only. Preserving the common scheme and continuity for a senior adult community necessitates the enforcement of age restrictions that prohibit children from becoming permanent residents in the community. Age restrictions are not constitutionally prohibited unless they are unreasonably or arbitrarily applied. Such restrictions are, however, governed by the Federal Fair Housing Act.[85] The Fair Housing Amendments Act of 1988 prohibits discrimination based upon age unless occupancy is intended for and restricted to persons 62 years of age or older, or when occupancy is restricted to residents 55 years of age or older and at least 80% of the parcels are occupied by at least one person 55 years of age or over.[86]

A community claiming senior-adult status is required to register with the Florida Commission on Human Relations, stating that the community complies with the appropriate requirements to qualify for the status. The filing must be submitted in writing on the letterhead of the community and signed by the association president. The registration must be renewed biennially from the date of the original filing. The Commission is authorized to charge a registration fee, not to exceed $20.00 for the filing, and the filings are public records and available in the Commission's Internet website. An administrative fine, not to exceed $500.00, may be imposed against a community that knowingly submits false information in its filing.[87]

---

[84]   *Laursen v. Giolli*, 549 So.2d 1174 (Fla. 2d DCA 1989).

[85]   *White Egret Condominium v. Franklin*, 379 So.2d 346 (Fla. 1979); *see Pomcrantz v. Woodlands Section 8 Ass'n*, 479 So.2d 794 (Fla. 4th DCA 1986); and *Rocek v. Markowitz*, *supra* note 1, applying *White Egret* to homeowners' associations.

[86]   42 U.S.C. §§3601-3619; *see also* §760.29 (4), F.S.

[87]   §760.29 (4)(e), F.S.

As with the enforcement of all restrictions, uniformity and consistency are important. Because age restrictions clearly have the potential of excluding persons from the community, adequate notice and timely enforcement must be consistently provided. Careful compliance with the Federal Fair Housing Act is also essential if an adult community is to be successfully preserved.

Deed restrictions and covenants restricting ownership or occupancy of a parcel based upon racial or religious grounds are not enforceable.[88] Any element of judicial enforcement of such a discriminatory covenant is considered "state action" and thus a violation of the Federal Civil Rights Act.[89]

7.9 Lease and Rental Restrictions. Many community governing documents contain restrictions for the lease and rental of parcels, and the association has the power and duty to enforce the restrictions.[90] Lease and rental restrictions that are clearly stated in the governing documents and uniformly enforced promote the residential character of the community and do not inherently violate any fundamental rights of the owner of the parcel.[91] When the rules or restrictions are unclear or when they are improperly applied, however, the objective may be lost. Tenants, guests and invitees of an owner occupying a parcel or using the common areas are required to comply with the governing documents of the community and the rules and regulations of the association.[92]

---

[88] *Harris v. Sunset Island Property Owners*, 116 So.2d 622 (Fla. 1959); *Shelley v. Kraemer*, 334 U.S. 1, 685 S.Ct. 836 (1948).

[89] 42 U.S.C. §1983; *see also Quail Creek Property Owners v. Hunter*, 538 So.2d 1288 (Fla. 2d DCA 1988).

[90] §720.303 (1), F.S.

[91] *Woodside Village Condominium v. Jahren*, 754 So.2d 831, 832 (Fla. 2d DCA 2000); *see also Woodside Village Condominium Assoc. v. Jahren*, 806 So.2d 452 (Fla. 2002) regarding amendments to rental restrictions.

[92] §720.305 (1), F.S.

7.10 Amendments to the Governing Documents. Because the governing documents establish the character and scheme for the community and the rights of those owning property in the community, there are restrictions on how the documents may be changed. Traditionally, the restrictions and the required vote for approving amendments to the articles of incorporation,[93] bylaws[94] and the declaration of covenants[95] are contained within the documents.

Where it is unclear from the documents whether an amendment can be adopted by the board of directors or requires approval by the membership, membership approval has been deemed necessary.[96] When the governing documents do not set forth the vote required for amendments, the law requires that an affirmative vote of two-thirds of the voting interests in the association be obtained. If the proposed amendment materially or adversely alters an owner's voting interests or increases the percentage by which a parcel shares in the common expenses, the owner and the record owners of liens on the affected parcel must join in the execution of the amendment.[97] When the required approval of the association membership specified in the documents and the law is attained, the amendment is validly enacted.[98]

---

[93]   §617.0202 (2) (b) and §617.1002, F.S.

[94]   §617.0206, F.S.; *see also Westwood Community Town Ass'n v. Lewis*, 687 So.2d 296 (Fla. 4th DCA 1997) holding that an amendment to bylaws cannot supersede provisions of the recorded covenants.

[95]   *Holiday Pines Prop. Owners v. Wetherington, supra* note 54; *see also Palma v. Townhomes of Oriole Ass'n, Inc.*, 610 So.2d 112 (Fla. 4th DCA 1992) and Isle of *Catalina Homeowners Ass'n, Inc v. Pardee*, 739 So.2d 664 (Fla. 5th DCA 1999).

[96]   *Palma v. Townhomes of Oriole Ass'n, Inc., supra* note 68.

[97]   §720.306 (1) (b) and (c), F.S.

[98]   *Holiday Pines Prop. Owners v. Wetherington, supra* note 54; *see also Zerquera v. Centennial Homeowners' Ass'n, Inc.*, 721 So.2d 751 (Fla. 3d DCA 1998).

If the developer has reserved the power in the declaration of covenants to amend or modify the restrictions governing the community, the power must be exercised in a reasonable manner so as not to destroy the general plan of development.[99] The developer may not use the "reserved power to amend" to prejudice the rights of parcel owners to use and enjoy the benefits of the common property without the consent of the owners.[100] Further, without the consent of all affected parcel owners, neither the developer[101] nor the association[102] is permitted to reduce the size of the common area or limit access of owners to it.[103]

7.11 Revival of the Governing Documents. The governing documents in some Florida homeowners associations provide for an expiration of the community covenants after a specified number of years. Residents in these communities have the option to revive the governing documents after the expiration date by following the procedural steps found in Chapter 720 of the Florida Statutes.[104]

A proposal to revive the community documents must be initiated by an organizing committee of not less than three (3) parcel owners in the community. The committee must prepare a complete set of the documents that are proposed for revival and identify the parcel owners to be subject to the revived documents. The proposed documents, together with a graphic depiction of the affected property must be presented to all of the affected owners by mail or hand delivery at least fourteen (14) days before approval of the revived documents is to be considered.[105]

---

99 *Id.*
100 *Blue Reef Holding Corp., Inc. v. Coyne*, 645 So.2d 1053 (Fla. 4th DCA 1994).
101 *Id.*
102 *Lewis v. S & T Anchorage, Inc.*, 616 So.2d 478 (Fla. 3d DCA 1993).
103 *S & T Anchorage, Inc. v. Lewis*, 575 So.2d 696 (Fla. 3d DCA 1991).
104 §§7 and 8, Chapter 2004-345, *Laws of Florida.*
105 §9, Chapter 2004-345, *Laws of Florida.*

A majority of the affected property owners may agree in writing to revive the governing documents, or the affected parcel owners may vote to revive the documents at a properly called membership meeting of the property owners. (See 2.4.) If the required approval is obtained at a membership meeting, the proof of notice of the meeting and the minutes of the meeting must be certified by an attorney or a court reporter.[106]

Once approved by a majority of the affected property owners, the governing documents and the documentation supporting the revival of the documents must be forwarded by the organizing committee to the Department of Community Affairs.[107] Once the Department determines that the proper procedures were followed, the organizing committee will be notified to record the revived community documents in the official records of the county where the property is located. The committee must thereafter deliver a recorded copy of the documents to all of the affected parcel owners. The revived governing documents are effective upon recording.[108]

7.12 Towing of Unauthorized Vehicles. The Florida Statutes impose specific requirements on a homeowners association or its designated representative prior to the towing of an improperly parked motor vehicle if the association is to avoid liability for its acts.[109] The owner of the improperly parked vehicle must personally be notified that parking is not authorized, or the area must be prominently posted at each driveway access within five feet of the public right of way line advising motorists that the area is a "tow-away zone." The notice on the signs must have light-reflective letters on contrasting background at least two inches in height, and the words "tow-away zone" must be

---

[106] §6, Chapter 2004-345, *Laws of Florida*.
[107] §10Chapter 2004-345, *Laws of Florida*.
[108] §11, Chapter 2004-345, *Laws of Florida*.
[109] §715.07 (2), F.S.

included on the signs in not less than four-inch letters. The sign structures must be at least four feet above ground level. If the homeowners' association has a contract with a towing company, the name and telephone number of the company must also appear on the sign.[110]

When an unauthorized vehicle is actually removed from the property in the community, it must be stored at a site within ten (10) miles of the property in a county having a population of more than 500,000 people and within fifteen (15) miles of the property in a county having a population of less that 500,000 people. The person towing the motor vehicle must notify the appropriate law enforcement officials within thirty (30) minutes of the towing and provide to them a description of the vehicle, the model and license plate number.

If the owner of the vehicle arrives at the scene prior to towing of the motor vehicle, the vehicle must be disconnected, and the owner shall be liable for the payment of a reasonable service fee. If the homeowners association causes a vehicle to be removed improperly, it is liable for the cost of removal, transportation and storage as well as damages resulting from the removal of the vehicle including any attorney's fees and court costs.[111]

7.13 Private Roadways. In communities that have private roadways, the association must operate and maintain the rights-of-way as required in the governing documents to avoid actions in law or equity resulting from their failure or refusal to carry out these responsibilities.[112] Associations also need to be sensitive to the fact that an accident or injury resulting from an

---

[110] §715.07 (2) (a), F.S.

[111] §715.07 (4), F.S.

[112] §720.305 (1), F.S.

improperly maintained roadway for which the association is responsible can expose the association and its membership to claims for damages for the association's negligence.[113] When permitted by the governing documents, the association may suspend the rights of a member to use the common areas for violation of the documents, but the suspension cannot impair the right of an owner or a tenant to have vehicular and pedestrian access to the owner's home, including the right to park a vehicle in permitted areas.[114] The association may authorize a city or county to exercise traffic control jurisdiction over the community's private roadways by written agreement. The agreement with a city or county must make provision for the costs of traffic control and liability insurance and may provide for the installation of multiparty stop signs and the regulation of access by means of security devices and personnel.[115]

If the roadways in a community are dedicated to the county and the homeowners desire to convert the roadways to private ownership, they may request the county to convey the roadways to the association. To make this change, the association must request the conveyance in writing and at least four-fifths of the owners must consent in writing. The county may then abandon the roads and convey them to the homeowners association for the purposes of converting the subdivision to a gated neighborhood with restricted public access to the roadways. The association must have the authority in the governing documents and must carry out the responsibility and agree to assume responsibility for the ongoing maintenance and repair of the roadways, as well as any drainage structures, street lighting and sidewalks. Upon conveyance from the county, the homeowners association holds the roadways in trust for the benefit of the owners of

---

[113] *National Title Insurance Co. v. Lakeshore I Condominium Assoc., Inc.,* 691 So.2d 1104 (Fla. 3d DCA 1997); *Winston Towers 100 Assoc., Inc. v. De Carlo,* 481 So.2d 1261 (Fla. 3d DCA 1986).

[114] §720.305 (1)(c), F.S.

[115] §316.006 (2)(b) and (3)(b), F.S.

property in the community and must operate and maintain the roadways for the use and benefit of the owners and their guests.[116]

7.14 Penny-ante Gambling. Unless prohibited by the governing documents, limited gambling is permitted in the common areas of the community or in an individual residence. Games permitted include poker, pinochle, bridge, rummy, canasta, hearts, dominoes and mah jongg. Jackpots are limited to $10 per game, the host must be present during the game and the host is not permitted to receive any commission. Participants may not be solicited to play and all must be over eighteen (18) years of age. No debt incurred in a game is legally enforceable. The homeowners association or an owner participating in the game shall not have any civil liability for damages if the restrictions of the law related to penny-ante gambling are properly followed.[117]

---

[116] §316.00825 (1), F.S.

[117] §849.093, F.S

8

Style and Format for Association Forms and Documents

Various types of formalities accompany the operation of the homeowners association. They ensure that proper procedures are followed to protect members' rights and that members are advised of the business and finances being conducted on their behalf. Implementing these formal prerequisites for association meetings, membership voting and actions by the directors is not complicated, but it is essential to the proper and successful operation of the association.

The forms and sample documents that follow in this chapter are designed to assist and guide those who are responsible for conducting the affairs of the homeowners association. They present the basic format for the formal documents that are used periodically by the association, and they can be adapted for use in most communities. When the bylaws of the association specify a different format or a variation in document content, the forms in this manual should yield to the requirements of the community's bylaws.

INDEX OF FORMS AND DOCUMENTS

**8.1   MEMBERSHIP MEETING FORMS AND
         SAMPLE DOCUMENTS**

Form 8.1-0 Notice of Meeting

Form 8.1-1 Proof of Notice Affidavit

Form 8.1-2 Agenda for Members Meeting

Form 8.1-3 General Proxy

Form 8.1-4 Limited Proxy

Form 8.1-5 Voting Certificate

Form 8.1-6 Minutes of Members Meeting

Form 8.1-7 Ballot for Board Election

Form 8.1-8 Roster of Parcel Owners

**8.2   BOARD OF DIRECTORS MEETINGS AND
         SAMPLE DOCUMENTS**

Form 8.2-0 Notice to Board Members

Form 8.2-1 Waiver of Notice by Board Members

Form 8.2-2 Notice of Board Meeting for
           Association Members

Form 8.2-3 Proof of Notice for Board Meeting

Form 8.2-4 Agenda of Board Meeting

Form 8.2-5 Written Action by Board Members

Form 8.2-6 Minutes of Board Meeting

Form 8.2-7 Official Records List

8.3   **OFFICER AND COMMITTEE FORMS AND
        SAMPLE DOCUMENTS**

Form 8.3-0 Registered Agent/Registered Office
        Designation

Form 8.3-1 Resolution Creating Committee
        of the Board

Form 8.3-2 Executive Declaration Creating Committee

Form 8.3-3 Committee Report

8.4   **BUDGET AND FINANCIAL FORMS
        AND SAMPLE DOCUMENTS**

Form 8.4-0 Budget

Form 8.4-1 Annual Financial Report

Form 8.4-2 Claim of Lien

Form 8.4-3 Satisfaction of Lien

8.5   **DISCLOSURE SUMMARY FOR
        PROSPECTIVE PURCHASERS**

Form 8.5-0 Disclosure Summary

CYPRESS HOMEOWNERS ASSOCIATION, INC.
A Corporation Not-for-Profit

NOTICE OF MEMBERS MEETING

NOTICE IS HEREBY GIVEN, in accordance with the Bylaws of the Cypress Homeowners Association, Inc., that the annual (special*) meeting of members will be held at the following date, time and place:

Date: January 15, 2006

Time: 7:00 p.m.

Place: Recreation Hall

Cypress Homeowners Association, Inc.
100 Cypress Lane
Cypress Springs, Florida 33444

Agenda:

1. Calling of roll and certifying of proxies.

2. Proof of notice of meeting or waiver of notice.

3. Reading and disposal of any unapproved minutes.

4. Election of inspectors of election.

5. Election of board members.

6. Reports of officers.

7. Reports of committees.

    a. Recreation Committee.

    b. Grounds Committee.

8. Unfinished business.

9. New business.

Form 8.1-0 Notice of Meeting

      a. Consideration of amendment to
         association bylaws.
      b. General discussion by members.

10. Adjournment.

CYPRESS HOMEOWNERS
ASSOCIATION, INC.

By:_____
      Secretary

Dated: This 20th day of December, 2005.

*(The notice for a special members meeting must state the purpose for which the meeting is called.)

CYPRESS HOMEOWNERS ASSOCIATION, INC.
A Corporation Not-for-Profit

PROOF OF NOTICE AFFIDAVIT

STATE OF FLORIDA

COUNTY OF PINELLAS

The undersigned Secretary of the Cypress Homeowners Association, Inc., being first duly sworn, deposes and says that notice of the annual (special) membership meeting was mailed or hand-delivered to each member at the address last furnished to the Association at least fourteen days prior to the annual (special) meeting.

Dated this 20th day of December, 2005.

_____
Secretary

The foregoing Affidavit was acknowledged before me this 20th day of December, 2005, by Nancy Thomas, the Secretary of Cypress Homeowners Association, Inc.

_____
Notary Public

My commission expires:

Form 8.1-1 Proof of Notice Affidavit

CYPRESS HOMEOWNERS ASSOCIATION, INC.
A Corporation Not-for-Profit

AGENDA

MEMBERSHIP MEETING

January 15, 2006

1. Calling of roll and certifying of proxies.

2. Proof of notice of meeting or waiver of notice.

3. Reading and disposal of any unapproved minutes.

4. Election of inspectors of election.

5. Election of board members.

6. Reports of officers.

7. Reports of committees.

   a. Recreation Committee.

   b. Grounds Committee.

8. Unfinished business.

9. New business.

   a. Consideration of amendments to association bylaws.

   b. General discussion by members.

10. Adjournment.

Form 8.1-2 Agenda for Members Meeting

CYPRESS HOMEOWNERS ASSOCIATION, INC.
A Corporation Not-for-Profit

PROXY

January 15, 2006

Membership Meeting

TO: Secretary

Cypress Homeowners Association, Inc.
100 Cypress Lane
Cypress Springs, Florida 33444

KNOW ALL PERSONS BY THESE PRESENTS, that the undersigned hereby appoints the Secretary of the Association or _____, attorney and agent with the power of substitution for and in the name, place and stead of the undersigned, to vote as proxy at the membership meeting of the Association, to be held at the Recreation Hall, January 15, 2006, at 7:00 p.m., and any adjournment thereof, according to the number of votes that the undersigned would be entitled to vote if then present upon the matters set forth in the Notice of Meeting dated December 20, 2004, a copy of which has been received by the undersigned.

(In no event shall this proxy be valid for a period longer than 90 days after the date of the first meeting for which it was given.)

Form 8.1-3 General Proxy

DATED this _____ day of January, 2006.

<u>Parcel Owner</u>

_____

_____

Parcel Number:_____
(or Property Address)

SUBSTITUTION OF PROXY

The undersigned, appointed as proxy above, does hereby designate _____ to substitute for me in the proxy set forth above.

Dated:_____   _____
                                              Proxy

CYPRESS HOMEOWNERS ASSOCIATION, INC.
A Corporation Not-for-Profit

PROXY

January 15, 2006

Membership Meeting

      KNOW ALL PERSONS BY THESE PRESENTS, that the undersigned hereby appoints the Secretary of the Association, his or her designee, or _____, attorney and agent with the power of substitution for and in the name, place and stead of the undersigned, to vote as proxy at the membership meeting of the Association, to be held at the Recreation Hall, January 15, 2006, at 7:00 p.m., and adjournment thereof, according to the number of votes that the undersigned would be entitled to vote if then present in accordance with the specifications hereinafter made, as follows:

General Powers

_____   I hereby authorize and instruct my proxy to use his best judgement on all matters which properly come before the meeting.

Limited Powers

_____   I hereby specifically authorize and instruct my proxy to cast my vote in reference to the following matters only as indicated below.

1.   Should the size of the board of directors be increased from 7 to 9 members?

      Yes_____   No_____

Form 8.1-4 Limited Proxy

2.   Should the bylaws of the Association be amended to provide that the terms of directors be for 2 years?

Yes_____   No_____

The undersigned ratify and confirm any and all acts and things that the proxy may do or cause to be done in the premises, whether at the meeting referred to above or at any change, adjournment or continuation of it, and revoke all prior proxies previously executed.

Dated:_____   Parcel Owner

Parcel Number:_____   _____

_____   _____

(or Property Address)

SUBSTITUTION OF PROXY

The undersigned, appointed as proxy above, does hereby designate _____ to substitute for me in the proxy set forth above.

Dated:_____   _____
                                                Proxy

(In no event shall this proxy be valid for a period longer than 90 days after the date of the first meeting for which it was given.)

Form 8.1-4 Limited Proxy

CYPRESS HOMEOWNERS ASSOCIATION, INC.
A Corporation Not-for-Profit

VOTING CERTIFICATE

TO: Secretary, Cypress Homeowners Association, Inc.
100 Cypress Lane
Cypress Springs, Florida 33444

KNOW ALL MEN BY THESE PRESENTS, that the undersigned are the record owners of that certain parcel in CYPRESS HOMEOWNERS ASSOCIATION, INC., shown below, and hereby constitute, appoint and designate _____ as the voting representative for the parcel owned by said undersigned pursuant to the Bylaws of the Association.

The aforenamed voting representative is hereby authorized and empowered to act in the capacity herein set forth until such time as the undersigned otherwise modifies or revokes the authority set forth in this voting certificate.

DATED this 1st day of December, 2005.

Parcel Owner

_____

_____

Parcel Number:_____

_____

(or Property Address)

Form 8.1-5 Voting Certificate

CYPRESS HOMEOWNERS ASSOCIATION, INC.
A Corporation Not-for-Profit

ANNUAL MEMBERS MEETING MINUTES

The meeting was called to order at 7:30 p.m., Monday, January 15, 2006, in the Recreation Hall by the President. The President announced that the first order of business was the calling of the roll and the certifying of the proxies. Upon its completion, it was announced that 100 members were represented in person and 50 members were represented by proxy. The President declared that a quorum of the 200 parcels was present.

The President next called upon the Secretary to present the affidavit for proof of notice and directed it to be annexed to the minutes of the meeting and made a permanent part of the Association's official records. The President stated that the next item of business was the reading of the minutes from the last members meeting. Upon a motion made by Mr. Jones and seconded by Mr. Smith, and upon discussion, it was unanimously carried by voice vote that the reading of the minutes be waived.

The next item of business was the appointment of inspectors of election. The President appointed the Association's Vice President, Sara Harris, and Mr. Campbell to serve as inspectors of election and directed that all ballots be turned over to the inspectors for tabulation. The President then stated that, without objection, the meeting would stand in recess until the tabulation of the ballots was completed.

Upon reconvening the recessed meeting, the President called upon the Vice President to announce the results of the election. The Vice President then stated that the following individuals were elected to serve for a term of one year on the Board of Directors:

Form 8.1-6 Minutes of Members Meeting

Joseph A. Jones

David Smith

Marc Wesley

The next order of business was the reports of officers and committees. The President recognized the Treasurer who gave the financial report for the preceding twelve months. Upon completion of the presentation, the President directed that it be annexed to the minutes of the meeting and distributed to the membership.

Under report of committees, the President recognized the Chairman of the Recreation Committee, Mr. Johnson, who presented the schedule of functions and events planned for the coming calendar year.

The President next asked for items of unfinished business. There being no unfinished business, the President then stated that the next item on the agenda was consideration of new business. Mr. Wesley moved that amendments to the bylaws be adopted. The motion was seconded, and, at the conclusion of the discussion, the amendments were approved by a vote of 138 yeas and 12 nays.

There being no further new business to come before the meeting and no further member seeking recognition, upon a motion duly made, seconded and unanimously carried, the President stated that the meeting was adjourned at the hour of 8:30 p.m.

_____

Secretary

Form 8.1-6 Minutes of Members Meeting

BALLOT

1. The following have been nominated to serve for a term of one year on the Board of Directors of the Homeowners Association. There are three vacancies on the Board of Directors and you may vote for up to three individuals by placing a check mark next to their names. A ballot voting for more than three individuals will be disallowed.

    Sara Harris   _____

    Joseph A. Jones   _____

    Matthew Marshall   _____

    David Smith   _____

    Marc Wesley   _____

2. Should the Bylaws of Cypress Homeowners Association, Inc., be amended to allow for directors to serve for a term of two (2) years in accordance with the full text of the proposed amendment which accompanied the mailing of the meeting notice?

    Yes_____   No_____

Form 8.1-7 Ballot for Board Election

CYPRESS HOMEOWNERS ASSOCIATION, INC.
A Corporation Not-for-Profit

ROSTER OF PARCEL OWNERS

PARCEL NUMBER	PARCEL OWNER	DESIGNATED VOTER
101	Sara Harris 101 Cypress Lane Cypress Springs, FL 33444 Tel. No. (111) 999-7101	Sara Harris
102	Matthew Marshall Amy Jo Marshall 102 Cypress Lane Cypress Springs, FL 33444 (no telephone)	Matthew Marshall
103	Peter Johnson Susan Johnson 103 Cypress Lane Cypress Springs, FL 33444 (telephone no. unknown)	Susan Johnson
104	David R. Smith Nancy H. Smith 104 Cypress Lane Cypress Springs, FL 33444 Tel. No. (111) 999-7104	David R. Smith

Form 8.1-8 Roster of Parcel Owners

105   Marc Wesley   Marc Wesley
            Chollet Wesley
            105 Cypress Lane
            Cypress Springs, FL 33444
            Tel. No. (111) 999-7105

106   ABP Corporation   David Dodd
            113 Main Street
            Cypress Springs, FL 33444
            Tel. No. (111) 999-7106
            Attn: David Dodd, Pres.

Form 8.1-8 Roster of Parcel Owners

CYPRESS HOMEOWNERS ASSOCIATION, INC.
A Corporation Not-for-Profit

NOTICE OF MEETING

TO: Members of the Board of Directors

1.   Sara Harris

2.   Ann Jones

3.   David Smith

4.   Marc Wesley

5.   Matthew Marshall

NOTICE IS HEREBY GIVEN that a meeting of the Board of Directors of Cypress Homeowners Association, Inc., will be held at the following date, time and place:

Date: January 16, 2006

Time: 9:00 a.m.

Place: Recreation Hall
         Cypress Homeowners Association, Inc.
         100 Cypress Lane
         Cypress Springs, Florida 33444

Dated: January 10, 2006

_____
Secretary

Form 8.2-0 Notice to Board Members

CYPRESS HOMEOWNERS ASSOCIATION, INC.
A Corporation Not-for-Profit

WAIVER OF NOTICE OF MEETING
OF BOARD OF DIRECTORS

We, the undersigned, being all of the members of the Board of Directors hereby agree and consent to the meeting of the Board to be held on the date and time, and at the place designated hereunder, and do hereby waive all notice whatsoever of such meeting and of any adjournment, or adjournments, thereof.

We do further agree and consent that any and all lawful business may be transacted at such meeting, or at any adjournment or adjournments thereof, as may be deemed advisable by the Board present thereat. Any business transacted at such meeting or at any adjournment or adjournments thereof, shall be as valid and legal and of the same force and effect as if such meeting, or adjourned meeting, were held after notice.

Place: Recreation Hall
Cypress Homeowners Assn., Inc.
100 Cypress Lane, Cypress Springs, FL 33444

Date: January 16, 2006

Time: 9:00 a.m.

Dated: January 10, 2006

_____   _____
Member, Board of Directors   Member, Board of Directors

_____   _____
Member, Board of Directors   Member, Board of Directors

Form 8.2-1 Waiver of Notice by Board Members

CYPRESS HOMEOWNERS ASSOCIATION, INC.
A Corporation Not-for-Profit

NOTICE TO ASSOCIATION MEMBERS OF
MEETING OF BOARD OF DIRECTORS

NOTICE IS HEREBY GIVEN that a meeting of the Board of Directors of Cypress Homeowners Association, Inc., will be held at the following date, time and place:

Place of Meeting: Recreation Hall
Cypress Homeowners
Association, Inc.
100 Cypress Lane
Cypress Springs, Florida 33444

Date of Meeting: January 16, 2006

Time of Meeting: 9:00 a.m.

Agenda:

The order of business for the regular meeting of the Board of Directors shall be:

1. Reading of minutes of the previous meeting.

2. Comment and discussion by parcel owners.

3. Report of Manager.

4. Report of Officers.

5. Unfinished business.

   a) Matters relating to grounds and buildings.

Form 8.2-2 Notice of Board Meeting for Association Members

  b) Matters relating to association financial affairs.

6. New business.

7. Adjournment.

This notice has been posted upon the property this 13th day of January, 2006, by order of the Board of Directors and in compliance with §720.303 (2), F.S.

Dated:_____   _____

           Secretary

Form 8.2-2 Notice of Board Meeting for Association Members

CYPRESS HOMEOWNERS ASSOCIATION, INC.
A Corporation Not-for-Profit

PROOF OF NOTICE AFFIDAVIT

STATE OF FLORIDA
COUNTY OF PINELLAS

Comes now the undersigned Secretary of Cypress Homeowners Association, Inc., being first duly sworn, deposes and says that said Secretary has posted or caused to be posted, conspicuously on the property, and has mailed or delivered or caused to be mailed or delivered written notice of the meeting of the Board of Directors to be held on January 5, 2006, not less than seven (7) days prior to said meeting.

Dated this 5th day of January, 2006

_____
Secretary

The foregoing Affidavit was acknowledged before me this 5th day of January, 2006, by Nancy Thomas, the Secretary of Cypress Homeowners Association, Inc.

_____
Notary Public

My commission expires:

Form 8.2-3 Proof of Notice for Board Meeting

CYPRESS HOMEOWNERS ASSOCIATION, INC.
A Corporation Not-for-Profit

AGENDA FOR REGULAR MEETING
OF THE BOARD OF DIRECTORS

The order of business for the regular meeting of the Board of Directors shall be as follows:

1. Reading of minutes of the previous meeting.

2. Comment and discussion by parcel owners on all matters to be considered by the Board.

3. Report of Manager.

4. Report of Officers.

5. Unfinished business.

   a) Matters relating to grounds and buildings.
   b) Matters relating to association financial affairs.

6. New business.

7. Adjournment.

Form 8.24 Agenda of Board Meeting

CYPRESS HOMEOWNERS ASSOCIATION, INC.
A Corporation Not-for-Profit

WRITTEN ACTION BY THE
BOARD OF DIRECTORS

The Board of Directors of Cypress Homeowners Association, Inc., determining that an emergency exists, and, by unanimous written action, adopts the following resolutions:

1.   RESOLVED, that the windstorm damage caused to the roof of the Recreation Building be repaired immediately to prevent further damage to the interior of the building.

2.   RESOLVED, that the President of the Association be and is hereby authorized and directed to obtain three bids and to accept the lowest responsible bid for the purpose of commencing the repairs to the roof of the Recreation Building.

3.   RESOLVED, that sufficient monies be made available from the reserve fund for the roof for the purpose of paying for the repair to the Recreation Building.

4.   RESOLVED, that a special meeting of the Board of Directors be called, after proper notice has been given and posted for the benefit of all the members, for the purpose of reviewing these written actions of the Board of Directors and for discussing further the wind damage to the association property.

Form 8.25 Written Action by Board Members

DONE by unanimous written consent this 16th day of January, 2006.

_____   _____
Member, Board of Directors   Member, Board of Directors

_____   _____
Member, Board of Directors   Member, Board of Directors

_____
Member, Board of Directors

CYPRESS HOMEOWNERS ASSOCIATION, INC.
A Corporation Not-for-Profit

MINUTES OF MEETING OF THE
BOARD OF DIRECTORS

The meeting of the Board of Directors was held on the date, time and at the place set forth in the notice of meeting fixing such time and place, and attached to the minutes of this meeting. Notice of the meeting was posted on the bulletin board in the Clubhouse forty-eight hours prior to the meeting.

There were present the following:
Joseph Jones
Ann Jones
Matthew Marshall
Sara Harris
David Smith

being all the members of the Board of Directors.

After the meeting was called to order, a motion was made, seconded and unanimously adopted waiving the reading of the minutes from the previous meeting. The President then declared that the floor was open for comment and discussion by any parcel owner on any subject that was to be considered by the Board or on any other subject concerning the homeowners association.

Mr. Wesley, 105 Cypress Lane, addressed the Board regarding safety in the swimming area. The President advised that the Board would review the matter in more detail. Mrs. Jones, 101 Cypress Lane, next addressed the Board on the speed of vehicles passing along the main entrance road to the community. The President directed that the manager notify the

Form 8.2-6 Minutes of Board Meeting

City and request that the roadway area be more closely patrolled.

At the conclusion of comments by parcel owners, the President called upon the property manager. The manager presented a report on the bids for insurance for the coming year and recommended that the lowest bid be accepted. Upon a motion duly made, seconded and unanimously carried, it was

> RESOLVED, that the bid of the Florida Insurance Company, being the lowest bid, be accepted and that they be directed to provide the insurance for the association property for the next calendar year.

The President stated that there were no reports of officers and no unfinished business. The President then asked if there was any new business to come before the meeting. There being no new business, and upon a motion duly made, seconded and unanimously carried, the President declared the same adjourned.

Dated: _____   _____
                                                        Secretary

Form 8.2-6 Minutes of Board Meeting

OFFICIAL RECORDS LIST

1.   Copy of the plans, specifications, permits, warranties and other items provided by the developer at the time of transition.

2.   Recorded copy of Declaration of Covenants and Restrictions of the Homeowners Association and all amendments.

3.   Copy of the Articles of Incorporation of the Association and all amendments.

4.   Copy of the Association Bylaws and all amendments.

5.   Copy of all current Rules and Regulations, Policy Statements and Resolutions of Procedure.

6.   Minutes for all meetings of the board of directors and of the membership for at least 7 years.

7.   Current roster of all parcel owners, their mailing addresses, voting certificates and, if known, telephone numbers.

8.   All current insurance policies for the Association.

9.   Management agreement, lease agreements and other contracts under which the Association is responsible.

10.   Bills of sale, deeds to common property, easements and other recorded documents.

Form 8.2-7 Official Records List

11.   Financial and accounting records for the Association and separate accounting records for any fees and charges for recreational amenities. The accounting records shall be maintained for at least 7 years and shall include but are not limited to:

    (a) Accurate, itemized and detailed records of all receipts and expenditures;

    (b) A current accounting for each parcel owner, with assessment amount, the amount paid and the balance due;

    (c) All audits, reviews, accounting statements and financial reports of the Association;

    (d) All contracts for work to be performed for the Association (bids shall also be considered official records and shall be kept for at least one year).

12.   Budget and annual financial report provided to the Association membership.

13.   All tax returns, financial statements and financial reports of the Association.

14.   All other records of the Association that identify, measure, record or communicate financial information.

Form 8.2-7 Official Records List

ACCEPTANCE OF APPOINTMENT OF REGISTERED AGENT AND DESIGNATION OF REGISTERED OFFICE

Pursuant to the provisions of Section 617.0501 and 617.0502, Florida Statutes, Cypress Homeowners Association, Inc., organized under the laws of the State of Florida, submits this statement for the purpose of changing its registered office and registered agent in the State of Florida as authorized by a resolution duly adopted by the Board of Directors on the 10th day of January, 2006, to the following:

JOSEPH JONES
101 Cypress Drive
Cypress Springs, Florida 33444

Date: _____   _____
                                                   Secretary

ACKNOWLEDGMENT

Having been named to accept service of process for the above stated corporation, at the place designated in this certificate, I hereby accept to act in this capacity, and agree to comply with the provisions of the law relative to keeping open said office.

Date: _____   _____
                                                   Registered Agent

Form 8.3-0 Registered Agent/Registered Office Designation

CYPRESS HOMEOWNERS ASSOCIATION, INC.
A Corporation Not-for-Profit

A RESOLUTION OF THE BOARD OF DIRECTORS CREATING A COMMITTEE OF THE BOARD TO SELECT AND RECOMMEND A MANAGER FOR THE HOMEOWNERS ASSOCIATION.

BE IT HEREBY RESOLVED by the Board of Directors of Cypress Homeowners Association, Inc., as follows:

Section 1. THAT a committee for the selection of a manager of the homeowners association is hereby created, and Joseph A. Jones, Nancy Thomas and David Smith are appointed to serve as members of the committee. Nancy Thomas shall serve as the chairman of the committee.

Section 2. THAT the committee shall have the authority to expend up to $500.00 in costs for advertisements and other related expenses in recruiting potential candidates for the position of manager.

Section 3. THAT the committee shall have the authority to investigate and interview candidates on behalf of the Board of Directors and shall select from the candidates the three individuals which the committee feels are best qualified to fill the position of manager and shall recommend them, in order of preference, to the full Board of Directors prior to the next regular quarterly meeting.

Form 8.3-1 Resolution Creating Committee of the Board

Section 4. THAT the committee shall not be authorized to hire any individual for the position of manager or otherwise expend, or commit to expend, any funds of the Association except as specifically authorized by this resolution.

ADOPTED by the Board of Directors this 10th day of January, 2006.

CYPRESS HOMEOWNERS ASSOCIATION, INC.

(CORPORATE SEAL)

By:_____
President

ATTEST:

_____
Secretary

CYPRESS HOMEOWNERS' ASSOCIATION, INC.
A Corporation Not-for-Profit

DECLARATION OF THE PRESIDENT

COMES NOW, Peter Johnson, President of Cypress Homeowners Association, Inc., and does hereby exercise the authority granted in the bylaws of the Association and does state and declare as follows:

1.   THAT, there is created a bylaw committee to study and evaluate the recent amendments to the law and to make a review of the bylaws of the Homeowners Association.

2.   THAT, the membership for the committee shall consist of Matthew Marshall, Marc Wesley and Sara Harris. Sara Harris is hereby designated to serve as chairman of the committee.

3.   THAT, the committee shall make recommendations for proposed amendments to the bylaws which govern the Homeowners Association and shall advise the President on any amendments to the law which may require changes to the policies and procedures of the Association.

4.   THAT, the committee shall not have the authority to act for or to bind the Homeowners Association nor shall it have the authority to expend any funds of the Association. The existence of the committee shall terminate upon submitting its final report to the President.

DONE this 30th day of September, 2006.

By:_____
President

Form 8.3-2 Executive Declaration Creating Committee

CYPRESS HOMEOWNERS ASSOCIATION, INC.
A Corporation Not-for-Profit

REPORT OF THE SPECIAL BYLAW COMMITTEE

TO: PRESIDENT AND MEMBERS OF THE
        BOARD OF DIRECTORS, CYPRESS
        HOMEOWNERS ASSOCIATION, INC.

FROM: SPECIAL BYLAW COMMITTEE, BY
        APPOINTMENT OF THE PRESIDENT
        SEPTEMBER 30, 2006

The special bylaw committee met on three occasions, after posting notice 48 hours in advance of each meeting, to evaluate the amendments to the law and to consider amendments to the Association's bylaws. As a result of the committee's study, the following changes are recommended:

1. The Association establish a standing committee for budget and finance.

2. The Association revise its fining policy to limit the amount to no more than $100.00.

3. The Association establish a uniform procedure for reviewing new owners and providing them copies of the governing documents.

The committee additionally recommends the following changes and additions be made to the bylaws of the Association:

1. Addition of a section to provide for voluntary binding arbitration of disputes between owners and the Association.

Form 8.3-3 Committee Report

2. Deletion of the section allowing members of the Board of Directors to abstain from voting.

3. Amendment to the section of the bylaws relating to the term of office for board members to permit members to serve for staggered terms of two years.

Respectfully submitted this 30th day of September, 2006.

_____
Chairman

_____
Member

_____
Member

CYPRESS HOMEOWNERS ASSOCIATION, INC.
A Corporation Not-for-Profit

2006 BUDGET

I. Expenses for the Association	Monthly	Annually
A. Administration of Association	$ 100.00	$ 1,200.00
B. Management Fees	702.00	8,424.00
C. Building Cleanup and Maintenance	100.00	1,200.00
D. Lawn and Property Maintenance	500.00	6,000.00
E. Rent for Recreation and Other Commonly Used Facilities	100.00	1,200.00
F. Expenses on Association Property		
1) Taxes	21.00	252.00
2) Cleaning and Maintenance	10.00	120.00
G. Taxes on Leased Property	10.00	120.00
H. Electricity	320.00	3,840.00
I. Water, Sewer and Garbage Service	900.00	10,800.00
J. Insurance	625.00	7,500.00
K. Miscellaneous		
1) Publication Subscriptions	2.00	24.00
2) Professional Services (legal and accounting)	100.00	1,200.00
L. Pest Control	100.00	1,200.00
TOTAL	$ 3,590.00	$ 43,080.00

Form 8.4-0 Budget

II. Reserves

A. Building Painting	$384.00	$ 4,608.00
B. Pavement Resurfacing	75.00	900.00
C. Roof Replacement	250.00	3,000.00
D. Miscellaneous Reserves	50.00	600.00
TOTAL	$ 759.00	$ 9,108.00

1. The balance in the reserve accounts of the Association at the beginning of the current budget year was as follows:

- a) Building painting $23,040.00
- b) Pavement resurfacing $7,200.00
- c) Roof replacement $24,000.00
- d) Miscellaneous reserves $3,000.00

2. The formula for each reserve category is based on the following estimates:

- a) Building painting to occur every 8 years and one-eighth of the total estimated cost is allocated to each fiscal year. Six of the eight years are currently on deposit.

- b) Pavement resurfacing to occur every 15 years and one-fifteenth of the total estimated cost is allocated to each fiscal year. Nine of the fifteen years are currently on deposit.

- c) Roof replacement to occur every 20 years and one-twentieth of the total estimated cost is allocated to each fiscal year. Eight of the twenty years are currently on deposit.

- d) Miscellaneous items of deferred maintenance and capital expenditures are based upon the needs for such expenditures as determined over the previous 10 years of the association and to cover needs not specifically identified in paragraphs (a), (b), and (c).

Form 8.4-0 Budget

CYPRESS HOMEOWNERS ASSOCIATION, INC.
A Corporation Not-for-Profit
2005 ANNUAL FINANCIAL REPORT

I. Expenses for the Association

	Expenditures	
	Budgeted	Actual
A. Administration of Association	$ 1,200.00	$ 1,200.00
B. Management Fees	8,424.00	8,424.00
C. Building Cleaning and Maintenance	1,200.00	1,200.00
D. Lawn and Property Maintenance	6,000.00	5,750.00
E. Rent for Recreation and Other Commonly Used Facilities	1,200.00	1,200.00
F. Expenses on Association Property		
1) Taxes	252.00	252.00
2) Cleaning and Maintenance	120.00	250.00
G. Taxes on Leased Property	120.00	120.00
H. Electricity (common elements)	3,840.00	2,910.00
I. Water, Sewer and Garbage Service	10,800.00	11,300.00
J. Insurance	7,500.00	7,489.00
K. Miscellaneous		
1) Publication Subscriptions	24.00	24.00
2) Professional Services (legal and accounting)	1,200.00	1,300.00
L. Pest Control	1,200.00	1,000.00
TOTAL	$ 43,080.00	$ 42,419.00

II. Income

A. Assessment Collection from Parcel Owners	$ 52,188.28
B. Interest Income from Operation Account	186.16
C. 2004 Surplus	210.12
TOTAL	$ 52,584.56

Form 8.4-1 Annual Financial Report

III. Summary

A. TOTAL INCOME	$ 52,584.56
B. TOTAL EXPENSES FOR OPERATIONS	-42,419.00
SUBTOTAL	$ 10,165.56
C. TOTAL RESERVE COLLECTIONS (2002)	-9,108.00
COMMON SURPLUS	$ 1,057.56

IV. Reserves

	Building Painting	Pavement Resurfacing	Roof Replacement	Misc Reserves
Beginning Balance	$ 16,996	$ 5,835	$ 25,200	$ 2,220
2005 Collections	4,608	900	3,000	600
Interest Earned	1,436	465	1,800	180
SUBTOTAL	$ 23,040	$ 7,200	$ 30,000	$ 3,000
2005 Expenditures	0	0	6,000	0
TOTAL RESERVES AT 2005 YEAR END	$ 23,040	$ 7,200	$ 24,000	$ 3,000

Form 8.4-1 Annual Financial Report

CLAIM OF LIEN
BY
CYPRESS HOMEOWNERS ASSOCIATION, INC.
A Corporation Not-for-Profit

STATE OF FLORIDA
COUNTY OF PINELLAS

In accordance with the authority of the Declaration of Covenants of Cypress Estates, CYPRESS HOMEOWNERS ASSOCIATION, INC., hereby claims a lien for all unpaid assessments now delinquent and hereafter accrued against the parcel and owner described below, in the initial amount and from the date stated, together with interest and reasonable attorney's fees and costs incident to the collection hereof, as follows:

Owner	Due Date	Assessment
Marc Wesley	June 15, 2006	$100.00

PROPERTY DESCRIPTION

Lot 5, CYPRESS ESTATES, according to map
or plat thereof recorded in Plat Book 8, Page
10, Public Records of Pinellas County, Florida.

EXECUTED this 15th day of July, 2006.

(CORPORATE SEAL)   CYPRESS HOMEOWNERS
                          ASSOCIATION, INC.

Form 8.4-2 Claim of Lien

ATTEST:

_____   By:_____
Secretary   President

    SWORN TO and subscribed before me this 15th day of July, 2006, by JOSEPH A. JONES, President, for the purpose therein expressed.

My commission expires: _____
                                  Notary Public

SATISFACTION OF LIEN
BY
CYPRESS HOMEOWNERS ASSOCIATION, INC.
A Corporation Not-for-Profit

STATE OF FLORIDA
COUNTY OF PINELLAS

FOR AND IN CONSIDERATION of a valuable sum in dollars, receipt of which is hereby acknowledged, the undersigned releases the lien recorded in Official Records Book 1000, Page 100, Public Records of Pinellas County, Florida, from the property owned by Marc Wesley and described as follows:

Lot 5, CYPRESS ESTATES, according to the map or plat thereof recorded in Plat Book 8, Page 10, Public Records of Pinellas County, Florida.

DONE AND EXECUTED this 23rd day of October, 2006.

(CORPORATE SEAL)   CYPRESS HOMEOWNERS
                      ASSOCIATION, INC.

ATTEST:

_____   By:_____
Secretary   President

On this 23rd day of October, 2006, personally appeared, JOSEPH A. JONES, President, and acknowledged that he executed this Satisfaction of Lien for the purpose therein expressed.

My commission expires: _____
                            Notary Public

Form 8.4-3 Satisfaction of Lien

DISCLOSURE SUMMARY
FOR
CYPRESS HOMEOWNERS ASSOCIATION, INC.

1. AS A PURCHASER OF PROPERTY IN THIS COMMUNITY, YOU WILL BE OBLIGATED TO BE A MEMBER OF A HOMEOWNERS ASSOCIATION.

2. THERE HAVE BEEN OR WILL BE RECORDED RESTRICTIVE COVENANTS GOVERNING THE USE AND OCCUPANCY OF PROPERTIES IN THIS COMMUNITY.

3. YOU WILL BE OBLIGATED TO PAY ASSESSMENTS TO THE ASSOCIATION. ASSESSMENTS MAY BE SUBJECT TO PERIODIC CHANGE. IF APPLICABLE, THE CURRENT AMOUNT IS $ _____ PER _____ . YOU WILL ALSO BE OBLIGATED TO PAY ANY SPECIAL ASSESSMENTS IMPOSED BY THE ASSOCIATION. SUCH SPECIAL ASSESSMENTS MAY BE SUBJECT TO CHANGE. IF APPLICABLE, THE CURRENT AMOUNT IS $_____ PER _____ .

4. YOU MAY BE OBLIGATED TO PAY SPECIAL ASSESSMENTS TO THE RESPECTIVE MUNICIPALITY, COUNTY, OR SPECIAL DISTRICT. ALL ASSESSMENTS ARE SUBJECT TO PERIODIC CHANGE.

5. YOUR FAILURE TO PAY THESE SPECIAL ASSESSMENTS OR ASSESSMENTS LEVIED BY A MANDATORY HOMEOWNERS ASSOCIATION COULD RESULT IN A LIEN ON YOUR PROPERTY.

6. THERE MAY BE AN OBLIGATION TO PAY RENT OR LAND USE FEES FOR RECREATIONAL OR OTHER COMMONLY USED FACILITIES AS AN OBLIGATION OF

Form 8.5-0 Disclosure Summary

MEMBERSHIP IN THE HOMEOWNERS ASSOCIATION. IF APPLICABLE, THE CURRENT AMOUNT IS

$ _____PER _____.

      7.   THE DEVELOPER MAY HAVE THE RIGHT TO AMEND THE RESTRICTIVE COVENANTS WITHOUT THE APPROVAL OF THE ASSOCIATION MEMBERSHIP OR THE APPROVAL OF THE PARCEL OWNERS.

      8.   THE STATEMENTS CONTAINED IN THIS DISCLOSURE FORM ARE ONLY SUMMARY IN NATURE, AND, AS A PROSPECTIVE PURCHASER, YOU SHOULD REFER TO THE COVENANTS AND THE ASSOCIATION GOVERNING DOCUMENTS BEFORE PURCHASING PROPERTY.

      9.   THESE DOCUMENTS ARE EITHER MATTERS OF PUBLIC RECORD AND CAN BE OBTAINED FROM THE RECORD OFFICE IN THE COUNTY WHERE THE PROPERTY IS LOCATED, OR ARE NOT RECORDED AND CAN BE OBTAINED FROM THE DEVELOPER.

DATE:_____   _____
                                      PURCHASER

                                        _____
                                      PURCHASER

Form 8.5-0 Disclosure Summary

Table of Cases

Pomerantz v. Woodlands Section 8 Association, 479 So.2d 794 (Fla. 4th DCA 1986).

Port Sewall Harbor & Tennis Club Owners Ass'n v. First Fed. Sav. & Loan, 463 So.2d 530 (Fla. 4th DCA 1985).

Powell v. Shumann Investments, Inc., 492 So.2d 850 (Fla. 1st DCA 1986).

Quail Creek Property Owners Ass'n v. Hunter, 538 So.2d 1288 (Fla. 2d DCA 1989).

Regency Highlands Associates v. Sherwood, 388 So.2d 271 (Fla. 4th DCA 1980).

Rocek v. Markowitz, 492 So.2d 460 (Fla. 5th DCA 1986).

Rolling Oaks Homeowners' Ass'n v. Dade County, 492 So.2d 686 (Fla. 3d DCA 1986).

Romero v. Shadywood Villas Homeowners Ass'n, Inc., 657 So.2d 1193 (Fla. 3d DCA 1995).

Roth v. Springlake II Homeowners' Ass'n, 533 So.2d 819 (Fla. 4th DCA 1988).

Royal Oak Landing Homeowners' Ass'n, Inc. v. Pelletier, 620 So.2d 786 (Fla. 4th DCA 1993).

S & T Anchorage, Inc. v. Lewis, 575 So.2d 696 (Fla. 3d DCA 1991).

Sanzare v. Varesi, 681 So.2d 785 (Fla. 4th DCA 1996).

Secret Oaks Owners' Ass'n v. D.E.P., 704 So.2d 702 (Fla. 5th DCA 1998).

Shelley v. Kraemer, 344 U.S. 1, 68 S.Ct. 836 (1948).

Shields v. Andros Isle Property Owners Ass'n, Inc., 872 So.2d 1003 (Fla. 4th DCA 2004).

Silver Blue Lakes Apts. v. Silver Blue Lakes Homeowners' Ass'n, 245 So.2d 609 (Fla. 1971).

Snead v. United States Trucking Corp., 380 So.2d 1075 (Fla. 1st DCA 1980).

Southwest Ranches Homeowners' Ass'n. v. County of Broward, 502 So.2d 931 (Fla. 4th DCA 1987).

Spring Hill Civic Ass'n v. Richard, 526 So.2d 211 (Fla. 5th DCA 1988).

Stiles v. Gordon Land Co., 44 So.2d 417 (Fla. 1950).

Stiller v. Mariner Cay Property Owners Ass'n, 513 So.2d 798 (Fla. 4th DCA 1987).

Strathmore Gate-East at Lake St. George Homeowners' Ass'n v. Levitt Homes, 537 So.2d 657 (Fla. 2d DCA 1989).

Taco Bell of California v. Zappone, 324 So.2d 121 (Fla. 2d DCA 1975).

Taylor Creek Village Ass'n v. Houghton, 349 So.2d 1219 (Fla. 3d DCA 1977).

Index

If you enjoyed reading this book, here are some other Pineapple Press titles you might enjoy as well. To request our complete catalog or to place an order, write to Pineapple Press, P.O. Box 3889, Sarasota, Florida 34230, or call 1-800-PINEAPL (746-3275). Or visit our website at www.pineapplepress.com.

Homeowners Association Manual—Fifth Edition by Peter Dunbar and Marc Dunbar. This manual provides a step-by-step explanation of the requirements for meetings, membership voting, and the necessary parliamentary procedures. It serves as a guide to help ensure that the association carries out its responsibilities fairly and effectively. In addition to the comprehensive text, there are 28 forms and sample documents—all you need to run an effective homeowners association. ISBN 1-56164-313-0 (pb)

Condominium Concept—Ninth Edition by Peter M. Dunbar, Esq. An updated, practical guide for officers, owners, and directors of Florida Condominiums. Written in clear, concise language, this has been an indispensable working tool for officers, directors, homeowners, managers, realtors, and attorneys since the first edition in 1986. Cross-referenced to the Florida Statutes. Includes 67 forms. ISBN 1-56164-326-2 (pb)

The Club Board Members Guide by John L. Carroll. Although written with private club members in mind, the common-sense solutions offered here apply to a much broader audience, especially those who oversee the running of a non-profit organization. Learn what to expect as a club board member, what your legal responsibilities are, how meetings should be handled. ISBN 1-56164-244-4 (pb)

Organizing Special Events and Conferences revised edition by Darcy C. Devney. A comprehensive handbook for anyone who has to produce a public event—from a school fundraiser to a national conference. Learn the tricks and techniques of the professional event organizer. For volunteers and paid staff alike, with step-by-step instructions, checklists, and schedules. Includes website information and e-mail addresses for fundraising associations, catalogs, directories, and publications. ISBN 1-56164-217-7 (pb)

Florida Law: A Layman's Guide—Fourth Edition by Gerald B. Keane. Newly revised and updated, this practical guide is for anyone who needs to know the basics of Florida law. It covers property, family, business, and criminal law in an easy-to-read style. ISBN 1-56164-290-8 (pb)

Florida Divorce Handbook—Fourth Edition by Gerald Keane. Reflects the most recent changes in family law in Florida. It offers an overview of the divorce process, introduces the basic vocabulary and legal concepts associated with divorce, and familiarizes you with what to expect if you are planning to divorce in Florida or if you are already divorced and have questions about your rights. ISBN 1-56164-291-6 (pb)